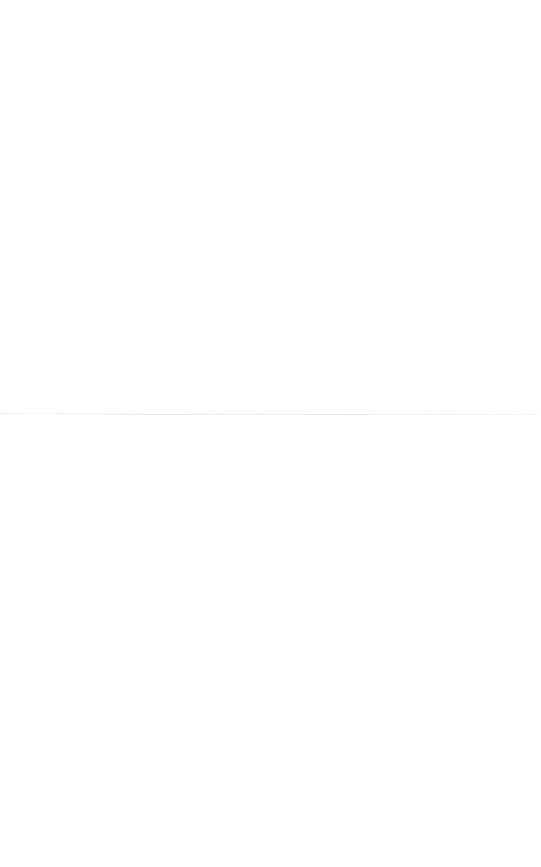

A Gift For:

_____

From:

_____

Date:

_____

Words in Due Season

Women of Grace Writers

WESTBOW
PRESS®
A DIVISION OF THOMAS NELSON
& ZONDERVAN

WestBow Press books may be ordered through booksellers or by contacting:

WestBow Press
A Division of Thomas Nelson & Zondervan
1663 Liberty Drive
Bloomington, IN 47403
www.westbowpress.com
1 (866) 928-1240

Group Photograph by Lynn Roehsler, Cochise County, AZ
Individual photograph submitted by author and used by permission.

ISBN: 978-1-9736-6958-6 (sc)
ISBN: 978-1-9736-6960-9 (hc)
ISBN: 978-1-9736-6959-3 (e)

Library of Congress Control Number: 2019909831

Print information available on the last page.

WestBow Press rev. date: 10/11/2019

Contents

Dedication xi

Preface...xiii

DEVOTIONS

Section 1:   **Peace** — Sonya Andres

1.   The Absence of Peace 3

2.   Open Altar...4

3.   Jealous 5

4.   Holy Bumps...6

5.   Who Wants to Prune You? —*Wannetta Wagner* 7

6.   Beautifully Written 8

7.   It's Just an Intersection 9

8.   From Pacemaker to Peacemaker 11

9.   Peace in the Battle —*David Ross Sherman*................................12

10.   "Where Are You Planted?"..13

11.   The Peace of God —*Diane Johnson* 14

12.   "Be All You Can Be"...15

13.   Fencing...16

14.   The Lighthouse 17

Section 2:   **Overwhelmed** — Carmen Mosher

1.   End-Of-The-Month Food..21

2.   Faith...22

3.   For Such A Time As This 23

4.   "I'm So Sorry, Mrs. Mosher"...24

5.   The Empty Freezer 25

6.   The Great Composer...27

7.   When You Come to The End of Yourself 28

8.   Blinded by The Light 30

9.   Boy, Oh Boy...31

10.   Burn, Baby Burn...32

11.   Dream Weaver 33

12.   I'm Not Letting Go 34

13.   Overshadowed 35

14.   Strength In Hiding..36

Section 3:   **Encouragement** — Millie Wasden

1.   Cinderella Girl 41
2.   The Quest 42
3.   First Baby Step 43
4.   Needy Me 44
5.   In the Pit 45
6.   God Uses Us Anyway 46
7.   Black Legs 47
8.   Listening to God 49
9.   Encouraged 50
10. Answered Prayer 51
11. Surviving Abuse —*Kristine Richardson* 52
12. Joy In Your Circumstances 53
13. God's Protection 54
14. Showing Forth God's Power 55

Section 4:   **Quiet** — Juanita Adamson

1.   Adoption Day 59
2.   Quiet Joy 60
3.   Don't Steal My Quiet! 61
4.   Wet Kiss 62
5.   Quiet—*Terry Hunt Crowley* 63
6.   Quiet the Mind 64
7.   Quiet Nature 65
8.   Impossible to Keep Quiet 67
9.   Quiet Is—*Cynthia Beckwith* 68
10. Weaned 69
11. Quietly Waiting —*Rosemary Raptis* 70
12. Study To Be Quiet 71
13. Smile 72
14. Addiction 73

Section 5:   **Music** — Paula J. Domianus

1.   Freedom 77
2.   The B - I - B - L – E 78
3.   In The Garden 80
4.   Let's Celebrate 81
5.   Power 82

6.   A Father's Love 83
7.   My Hero 84
8.   Heavenly Mission 86
9.   Sing Praises to His Greatness —*Rev. Rebecca J. Fiedler* 87
10. A Matter Of Minutes 88
11. Quest 89
12. The Little Chatterbox 91
13. In Her Room 92
14. Follow Me 93

Section 6:   **Watch** — Phyllis Andrews

1.   Watch 97
2.   Final Approach Into Tucson 98
3.   Watch the Pot 99
4.   In the Fulness Of Time 100
5.   What Is Man? 101
6.   Beauty Marks 102
7.   Can You Come Help Us? 103
8.   For Heaven's Sake 105
9.   Guard Your Heart 106
10. Not on My Watch 107
11. God Has Forgotten Me? —*Alan Reed* 108
12. Watch Your Mouth 109
13. P.I.P. 110
14. I See You 112

Section 7:   **Understanding** — Karen Furukawa

1.   Nuggets of Understanding 117
2.   Perspective 119
3.   To the Very End 120
4.   A Soft Power 121
5.   Tree-Of-Life Words —*Sharon Rustia* 122
6.   Remnant 123
7.   Willing to Dig? 124
8.   In Good Standing 126
9.   See —*Olivia Brant* 127
10. The Right Hand of God 128
11. Mary Understood Differently —*Pat Olson* 129
12. May His Face Shine Upon You 130

13.   Our Enemy 131
14.   Change 132

Section 8:   **Found** — Audrey Rierson

1.   The Absence of Sound 137
2.   Great Artisan 138
3.   Perfectly Planned 139
4.   Possible or Impossible? 141
5.   Christmas Box 143
6.   God's Covenant 145
7.   The Wonderful Pacifier 146
8.   Food for The Soul 149
9.   Arizona Sunset 151
10.   Best Gift Ever 152
11.   A Life Well Lived 154
12.   Divine Commitment 156
13.   The Prayer Diet 158
14.   What Would You Do? 159

Section 9:   **Endurance** — Catherine Ricks Urbalejo

1.   That Thing (Plugged Up) 163
2.   Enduring the Fiery Furnace 164
3.   Patient Endurance 165
4.   Cloud of Witnesses 166
5.   Hold Firm 167
6.   Row, Row, Your Boat 168
7.   The Key 169
8.   Enduring Discipline 172
9.   Angles and Tangles 173
10.   Trust and Obey 174
11.   Poisonous Fangs 175
12.   Armageddon Within 176
13.   Ultimate Endurance – Our Role Model 177
14.   Words in Due Season 178

Women of Grace Writers 179
Contributing Authors 181
End Notes 185

Dedication

IN LOVING MEMORY OF NAOMI Elaine LINDSEY
September 22, 1980 – October 10, 2017

Naomi was taken from this earthly realm too soon. There was so much more she desired to do, so many more who she wanted to impact with the love of her Lord and Savior Jesus Christ.

Naomi was a worshipper, pure and simple. She would enter the presence of Jesus with a pure, childlike abandon, face and arms lifted to heaven with smile and song upon her lips. Like most of us, Naomi was no stranger to struggles. But it was through those struggles that she drew into closer intimacy with her One True Love. She had learned to lean upon the Master in every way. The struggles constant and the pain real, and yet, Naomi's faith in her Savior remained stable, and her joy was always evident.

Naomi's life is truly "a word in due season."

It is a word that assures us of how much God's love continually surrounds us, even as we struggle with the complexities of life.

Therefore, we dedicate this collection of writings to her memory in hopes that we all might be inspired by her example of joy through trials. It is our prayer that through these humble compositions we all might pursue the Savior with passionate abandon as Naomi did -- confident that heaven and the presence of Jesus will be worth it all.

See you soon, Naomi!

Preface

"A man has joy by the answer of his mouth,
And a word spoken in due season, how good it is!"
Proverbs 15:23 *(NKJV)*

Peace

Peace by the world is defined by human wisdom. It is broken just like the symbol used internationally for peace and has been called the broken cross. I lived by the world's definition of peace for many years.

Peace by God's definition is unbroken and is here for eternity. The symbol for God's peace is the cross that His Son Jesus died on. Today I choose to live in the freedom of God's peace; it is the ultimate gift. He has given me.

God gave me the word peace to write about two years ago. Honestly, I didn't know why until now. A few months ago, a friend asked me why my word was peace. My answer was that I had too many "little-broken pieces" of life still in my heart. God took a thread and cross stitched the brokenness together with HIS peace that surpasses ALL understanding.

> *"Make every effort to keep the unity of the Spirit through the bond of peace."* Ephesians 4:3 (NIV)

Do you need God's peace to dwell in your heart? I pray that the Holy Spirit will help you feel God's peace in the first section of our book.

Shalom

The Absence of Peace

"Peace I leave with you. My peace I give to you. I do not give peace to you as the world gives. Do not let your hearts be troubled or afraid."
John 14:27 (NIV)

D*ivine Will* [1] was a movie filmed in Punkyville, Kentucky. Will Blessing caused lots of trouble in the city, so Dave, his uncle, decided to accept a job in this small town. Life there had always been out of the ordinary. Dave, a former rock star, would now be the church's new choir director. The choir begins to thrive with Dave's able leadership and Will as a singer with them.

Besides singing, Will had another divine gift and mysteriously began to change the town. Punkyville becomes a town of music and miracles intertwined with faith and love. Will's mother had always told him he had a divine gift.

The people Will Blessing touched would instantly be filled with God's peace. You could see light energy (Holy Spirit) in his hand as he touched someone's hand. That person began to desire what Will had, Jesus. The acting wasn't good. The movie was lame, and after 20 minutes, I reached to shut it off. However, something stopped me, and I watched the entire movie before going to bed. At 2 a.m. the next morning, I woke up thinking about the movie. I walked out to the living room feeling restless; God whispered a word to me—Peace.

You will fill yourself with My Word and touch my people with peace! I was so excited! Yes, I can see myself doing that! Off to bed, I went and halfway down the hall I believe God spoke, there is an absence of peace in your heart. *Remember your circumstances in the last year sometimes you had My Peace. You held some situations on your heart without me. A trial for you filled your mind with overwhelming anxiety. Your circumstances do not matter, and My Peace always needs to dwell in your soul.*

My feelings about the movie are not crucial because God acted mysteriously once again. I will keep **P** (Pursuing) **E** (Everlasting) **A** (Amazing) **C** (Christlike) **E** (Endeavors). God is the Prince of Peace. His Divine Will for us is always to be at peace. HIS peace that surpasses all understanding.

—Sonya Andres

Open Altar

*"May the God of hope fill you with all joy and peace as you trust in him,
so that you may overflow with hope by the power of the Holy Spirit."*
Romans 15:13 (NIV)

The Calvary First Assembly of God in Stockton, CA, has an "Open Altar" policy. During worship by the leading of the Holy Spirit, you can move freely to the altar for praising and prayer. One Sunday morning, as I was worshipping God, my heart starts beating faster. For me, this was a sign from God to go up front to the altar. As I moved forward, God led me to believe there was a woman in our midst, who had a heavy heart. Raising my hands and worshipping, I cried out to God in supplication for this person. I expected that this lady would come to the altar and pray with me. Much to my surprise when the worship music ended, no one came. On the way back to my seat, I started to question God, and then I saw a lady weeping profusely. I sat down by her and wrapped my arms around her. She repeated several times, "I should of went to the altar, I should of went to the altar. God wanted me to go." When I shared with her that it was okay and that God still loved her, it brought some peace into her heart. The kicker that gave her total peace was when I assured her that next Sunday if God wanted her to go to the altar, we would go together.

Can you guess what happened next Sunday? God led us to the altar. Her prayer request was about her daughter. The Holy Spirit encouraged me to have her pray for herself. My hands took her hands and lifted them high unto the Lord.

You don't need a physical altar to worship God. After reading this devotion, lift your hands and praise God right where you are! Let God open your heart by altering it! His altar is always open!

—Sonya Andres

Jealous

"We demolish arguments and every pretension
that sets itself up against the knowledge
of God, and we take captive every thought to make it obedient to Christ."
2 Corinthians 10:5 (NIV)

One morning I was sitting in our ladies Bible study, listening intently to the teaching. A thought came to me—*you should be jealous of her; you should be jealous of her.* It wasn't anything about one lady; it was coming at me after several of them made responses. *What? Jealous*, I thought! *Why? These ladies are my sisters in Christ.*

I laid my head back on the couch and looked up to the massive wall in front of me. I could see one word, JEALOUS! Yes, it was J E A L O U S, and it was huge! *WAIT, STOP THE PRESSES! What is going on in my head!* Suddenly, I realized that it was Satan trying to distract me from what God was pouring into my heart!

God reminded me to take that thought captive and that He delivered me of the jealousy spirit years ago. After Scott and I first got married, the spirit of jealousy shot out of me in several areas of my life—but it was most intense with his daughter, Brooke. Our marriage was in trouble! Scott told me I had to change as it was pushing us further apart. God's timing was so incredible!

During a women's retreat, I could see Jesus walking around the room touching other women! *Okay, God, PLEASE help me.* Suddenly I was set free! It was like I visualized a piece of paper coming out of my body (like pulling out a fortune from a cookie) that read JEALOUS!! The sheet of paper descended into the air, and my spirit was free.

As I looked up, I saw the word, JEALOUS! But it no longer called to me. I realized that taking those thoughts into captivity in obedience to Christ was the key to my freedom. The Bible study continued—my heart at peace.

—Sonya Andres

Holy Bumps

*"I want to know Christ—yes, to know the power of his resurrection
and participation in his sufferings, becoming like him in his death,
and so, somehow, attaining to the resurrection from the dead."*
Philippians 3:10-11 (NIV)

The Women of Grace Writers 2017 2-day retreat's theme was "The Me God Sees—A Reflection of His Purpose and Plan." The anticipation of attending a retreat is always exciting. It's time away from the ordinary things in life that can consume you daily—time with ladies who are fellow believers and have become lifetime friends—time to help you focus on Jesus Christ.

As I was driving to the retreat, I thought about how God sees me, and then I looked up into the dark sky. It was one cloudy and raining kind of day! My thoughts were focused on if I had everything done. Goosebumps of anxiety filled my arms—it is my job to take care of my household, and all the women things, we women do.

I wondered what the other ladies were thinking about as they approached the retreat destination. I prayed a short prayer asking God to help me see me—as he sees me.

We are all evangelists, and we must take the Word to the world. "Then He [Jesus] said to *them* all, 'If anyone desires to come after Me, let him deny himself, and take up his cross daily, and follow Me'" Luke 9:23 (NKJV).

The Friday night session ended with our coordinator asking us to help carry the life-size cross. My hand reached out and touched the cross. The Power of the Holy Spirit penetrated my hand and consumed my entire body. HOLY BUMPS! Peace in its entirety. When we got to the top of the treehouse, all I could think about was the word resurrection. Resurrection means rising from the dead. Believers are united in Christ by the trust. The Spirit regenerates our lives. The only way to know the resurrection victory is to apply the crucifixion personally. Die to sin and rise. Jesus Christ will show you the person God wants you to be.

Saturday morning driving back to the retreat, the sky was clear— God had calmed our storms. He had turned my goosebumps into "Holy Bumps"—**PEACE!**

—Sonya Andres

Who Wants to Prune You?

"For you shall go out with joy, and be led out with peace;
The mountains and the hills shall break forth into singing before you.
And all the trees of the field shall clap their hands.
Instead of the thorn shall come up the cypress tree,
And instead of the brier shall come up the myrtle tree;
And it shall be to the LORD for a name,
For an everlasting sign that shall not be cut off."
Isaiah 55:12,13 (NKJV)

There was a beautiful tree in the backyard. It was full and provided privacy and shade, yet someone felt that too many suckers and limbs were growing on it and took it upon themselves to prune it! Not only was it pruned, but all the branches that fell to the ground were left there to wither and die—in the heat—it left a trail of ugly. Will the tree grow back and be beautiful again? Yes! Unless it was a tree that could only be pruned in a certain season.

It is so true that we have things that need to be pruned out, so we can grow and do all God has for us. The key is allowing God to do the pruning. Have you experienced pruning in life that you didn't ask for and it just left a mess? The pruning wasn't necessary, but someone went gung-ho, thinking it was the right thing to do.

Who is pruning the things in your life? It is the job of the Holy Spirit, yet so many times we try to play that role, or someone plays it for us. Depending on our response, it could be a matter of life and death. When we respond with a right heart attitude, knowing the process is essential to our growth, we come to a place of peace.

When it's of God, the Holy Spirit comes and cleanses us, and there is no mess left because HE is doing a new thing, all for HIS eternal glory!

How beautiful it is when the Holy Spirit—the master pruner—comes alongside to mend and heal, giving us peace during HIS pruning process.

It's amazing what you can learn from a tree!

—Wannetta Wagner

Beautifully Written

"Your beauty should not come from outward adornment,
such as elaborate hairstyles and the
wearing of gold jewelry or fine clothes. Rather, it should
be that of your inner self, the unfading beauty
of a gentle and quiet spirit, which is of great worth in God's sight."
1 Peter 3:3,4 (NIV)

Beauty is in the eye of the beholder.

What is a beholder? A beholder is someone who gains awareness of things through the senses, especially sight. If beauty is in the eye of the beholder, then the person who is observing gets to decide what is beautiful. "Beauty is in the eye of the beholder" is a common saying meaning that beauty doesn't exist on its own but by observers.

A friend of mine had shared with me that if you only write one devotion and touch just one lady with it, wouldn't it be worth it? It's as if time stood still as I let that resonate in my heart. The conversation kept coming up into my mind and convincing me that I could write one devotion.

I joined Women of Grace Writers and wrote two devotions that were so dear to my heart—published in our book, *Mountains of Grace*.

My friend was a beholder! The reason she could see that in me is that she knows the greatest BEHOLDER of all, God. She is a gentle and quiet spirit. She loves Him and reflects the beauty of God.

"Wouldn't it be worth it?" Yes, it sure is. My writing abilities continue to grow and touch the lives of many others. One of my writings touched the heart of a lady, who was in a similar situation as a caregiver for her parent. She looked at her circumstance through God's eye's because of how God inspired me to write it. When we write God's words, they become beautifully written. I am off to write another devotion.

So, what about you? If you could touch one lady's heart with writing a devotion—perhaps, to bring her peace in her situation. Wouldn't it be worth it?

—Sonya Andres

It's Just an Intersection

"Stand at the crossroads and look; ask for the ancient paths,
ask where the good way is, and walk in it, and you will find rest
for your souls. But you said, 'We will not walk in it.'"
Jeremiah 6:16 (NIV)

Scott and I were driving down Fry Blvd, Sierra Vista, AZ. My heart was pounding, and I gasped for a breath of air. My eyes looked up, and there we were at the intersection of Fry Blvd and Coronado Dr. My legs started to quiver. Scott sensed something was wrong and asked me to explain. I said this is where it happened. Calmly he responded, "It's just an intersection." *What a weird thing to say*, I thought. My mind went back to June 30, 2015, just a few months before. This crossroad was where my momma passed away, and my life has never been the same. What did my momma think about that day? She was happy because Dad was taking her to coffee at one of her favorite places. She had no clue that God ordained that day when He would take her to heaven. Some people call it an accident, but it was God's plan. He knew that they would be driving and crossing through this road. Yes, this is an intersection of life!

This day reminded me of the prophet Samuel in 1 Samuel 7:12 (NIV)—*"Then Samuel took a stone and set it up between Mizpah and Shen. He named it Ebenezer, saying, "Thus far the LORD has helped us."*

The Hebrew word Ebenezer means "stone of help." "My stone of help," says "Rosie's Corner" named after my precious momma, inscribed in a beautiful cloud above the Fry and Coronado crossroad. It is my Ebenezer. It's where my momma parted from this earth into eternity.

My mom helped me in my life so many times. God has taken a trial and turned it into a blessing. Now I drive through Rosie's Corner with HIS peace that surpasses all understanding.

Are you at a crossroad? Look to the God of Peace.

—Sonya Andres

EXPECT PEACE AT THE CROSSROADS OF YOUR LIFE

From Pacemaker to Peacemaker

"Peacemakers who sow in peace reap a harvest of righteousness."
James 3:18 (NIV)

Scott and I started reminiscing about God implanting a pacemaker to help my heart. The electrical part of my heart was broken. My mind wandered back to March 7, 2012, and how God had every little detail planned. As Scott drove me to the emergency room, I said to him, "God wants me to speak to a lady about HIM." From that moment on, my focus was on God's plan and I started searching for that lady! Wow! There were so many ladies in the ER! I kept asking God, is this her, is that her?

After four hospitals, two ambulance rides, Scott sleeping on a five-foot-long sofa with him being 6 ft 8 and my girls flying to California to see me, God finally showed me the lady. Of course, it had to be in God's timing!

There she was! She was my ICU nurse. She looked at me and couldn't believe how peaceful I was. I said, "You are the one!"

She said, "What?" "I believe God wants me to speak to you about Him." My new friend was changed that day. God used me to get her focus back on HIM. You see, she had driven from Atlanta, Georgia, to take this temporary job, and I was one of her first patients. God allowed me to encourage His precious daughter.

I was recovering from my surgery for a pacemaker God used me as a peacemaker for the ICU nurse and blessed me beyond measure with His PEACE.

Do you need a change of pace to get your focus back on HIM?

—Sonya Andres

Peace in the Battle

"Be anxious for nothing, but in everything by prayer
and supplication, with thanksgiving, let your
requests be made known to God; and the peace of God,
which surpasses all understanding, will
guard your hearts and minds through Christ Jesus."
Philippians 4:6-7 (NKJV)

There are times in our lives that are filled with such turmoil that peace seems to evacuate first and leave us completely. As I watched my wife cling to life after a 5-hour surgery for stage IV ovarian cancer, this was such a time for me. I didn't even know she had a stroke during the surgery, but she refused to wake up and more doctors were called in to see why.

As I prayed by her bedside, crying out to God to heal her, watching her in an unconscious state, peace began to overwhelm me and take from me every vestige of doubt, care, and frustration that had crept into my soul. I was at a loss as to why God would give me this peace during this time of total confusion. I began to immediately praise God for His goodness as I felt the hand of God enter into the situation. I ran down to the hospital chapel and started to sing praises to the Lord. I was filled with joy as I felt the peace of God remove all doubt. I felt the assurance that she would be healed. She spent 40 days in the hospital. It has been seven years, and she has been fully restored. Sometimes it is necessary to let our faith and prayers bring our peace. Paul, the author of Philippians 4:6-7 (NKJV) knew when he wrote the words.

As we move from that faith to that peace, the phenomenon of joy will most certainly occur. It is that joy that accompanies things of God. As you rest in His peace, His joy will overwhelm you as you are comforted by the knowledge that the God of heaven has heard you.

—David Ross Sherman

"Where Are You Planted?"

"And the peace of God, which transcends all understanding, will guard your hearts and your minds in Christ Jesus."
Philippians 4:7 (NIV)

Love your neighbor as yourself means to love people unconditionally with a sincerity straight from the heart. A couple of years ago we heard a sermon called "Bloom Where You Are Planted." Scott and I took this to heart. In the neighborhood where God planted us, our neighbors see and feel the inner peace God has given us. Our neighbors have our phone numbers. They are free to call us especially when in need. We have provided food, maintenance on their homes, taken them to appointments, and, most importantly, prayed and witnessed to them.

One morning we woke up to a police officer ringing our doorbell. He asked us if we knew that someone had stolen the tires on Scott's truck. We said, "No!" I walked out to the vehicle and just started laughing—it looked so funny parked on the street without tires. During the night, a thief came and stole all the tires but left his jack. The police officer wrote up the incident. As we walked back into our house, Scott and I prayed for the person who took the tires. Later that day, the officer came to see if he could get any DNA to catch the thief. He said, "It didn't look good." Scott sensed something was wrong with the policeman and asked to pray for him for peace in his situation. The officer's eyes teared up. He was having marital issues. As the officer left, he seemed less troubled and more at peace.

We will continue to love and pray for our neighbors, asking God to bless their homes with His peace, as He fills ours. We continue to bloom where we have been planted.

—Sonya Andres

The Peace of God

*"I am leaving you with a gift—peace of mind and heart. And the peace
I give is a gift the world cannot give. So, don't be troubled or afraid."*
John 14:27 (NLT)

When we think about the Christian life and the trust we are called to have in Christ, one of the biggest benefits or blessings of that relationship is His amazing peace—that overwhelming knowledge and awareness that He is in control, regardless of the situation. How is that possible to have that peace that surpasses all understanding when the doctor says, "It's terminal," when your spouse says, "I'm done," a child becomes a prodigal, when your career comes to a sudden stop, when someone has maligned you, or when dark days seem to settle in like an unwanted season? How can we have God's peace if peace is "the freedom of disturbance, quiet and tranquil?"

Christ's answer is the same answer today as the day He gave it to His disciples when He was preparing for the cross. He told them to believe in Him, trust in Him. Know without a shadow of a doubt that He is always present.

Oh, your circumstances may not change my friend, but to experience His peace—your focus must change. Peace is the byproduct of knowing He has every situation in His hands. Life's circumstances have not taken Him by surprise, so there is nothing in this world we cannot entrust to Him. There is nothing He can't get us through, and He will show us His majesty in the middle of it.

—Diane Johnson

"Be All You Can Be"

*"You then, my son, be strong in the grace that is in Christ Jesus. And the
things you have heard me say in the presence of many witnesses entrust to
reliable people who will also be qualified to teach
others. Join with me in suffering,
like a good soldier of Christ Jesus. No one serving as a soldier gets entangled
in civilian affairs, but rather tries to please his commanding officer."*
2 Timothy 2:1-4 (NIV)

"**B**e All You Can Be" was the US Army's recruiting slogan for over 20 years.
Earl Carter created this theme in 1980 and was the longest-lived slogan the
Army ever had. It demonstrated that one could be all you could be in several
ways by learning a skill, earning college money, and by serving your country.
Military service helped young people succeed when returning to civilian life.

Todd Nelson, a friend who was in the Army, took his position with the
utmost respect. However, his assignment from the Lord was taken even more
seriously.

When Todd was overseas, he was struck by an IED. In the incident, Todd
lost an eye, ear, and most of the skin on his face. He had multiple injuries that
led him to 48+ surgeries over the next few years.

It was an amazing test of faith for Todd and his wife, Sarah. The Army
flew him to Texas where Sarah went to be with him. His physical body was in
bad shape, but his spiritual mind was at peace with the Lord. Todd's spirit was
ALIVE in Jesus Christ! Today, Todd helps other veteran's find peace through
their tragic circumstances.

Todd didn't go to heaven that day. When He does, I can imagine them
folding his flag—one-fold, two-fold (Todd's belief in eternal life), and third
fold. The fourth fold reminds me of Todd's trust in God in times of peace
as well as His divine guidance in times of war. To a Christian citizen, the
twelfth fold symbolizes eternity and glorifies God, the Father, the Son, and
the Holy Ghost. The last fold reminds us of our national motto "IN GOD WE
TRUST"—God whispers to Todd, "Well done, good and faithful servant."

"Be All You Can Be in God's Army"

—Sonya Andres

Fencing

*"Put on the full armor of God, so that you can take
your stand against the devil's schemes."*
Ephesians 6:10 (NIV)

Fencing started in 1896 as an organized sport using a sword called a foil or sabre. Fencers learn to attack and defend by training with a set of movements and rules.

Fencers must understand the rules, dress safely, and equip themselves appropriately. They must put on sports underwear, long socks, breeches, sports shoes, plastic chest protector, underarm protector, a jacket with a strap between the legs, body cord, a lame' (a vest for the target area), and a protective mask.

Although believers can relate to the preparation of a fencer, our armor is not physical but spiritual. Believers must understand the Bible, dress safely, and equip themselves properly. Each day they must put on the full armor of God including buckling the Belt of Truth, the Breastplate of Righteousness, the Shoes of the Gospel of Peace, the Helmet of Salvation, and carry the Shield of Faith and the Sword of the Spirit.

Fencers use their physical swords for sport—believers use their spiritual swords to break down the strongholds of adultery, uncleanness, lasciviousness, idolatry, witchcraft, hatred, variance, wrath, strife, seditions, heresies, envying, drunkenness, etc.

Believers use their swords to enjoy love, joy, peace, longsuffering, gentleness, goodness, faith, meekness, and temperance.

For fencers to win tournaments, they must not only dress appropriately but must train all the time.

To "take your stand against the devil's schemes" and bask in God's peace, believers must never neglect the study of His Word, prayer, and the donning of the Armor of God daily.

Are you wearing your appropriate clothing?

—Sonya Andres

The Lighthouse

*"I am the light of the world. Whoever follows me will
never walk in darkness, but will have the light of life."*
John 8:12 (NIV)

I stand at the foundation of the lighthouse and look up at the bright light beaming over me. I enter the structure and find a spiral staircase, that seems endless as I begin my ascent. The light beckons me to my destiny as I climb round and round, step by step.

Each step I take reminds me of my life's journey. I come to each window and look out. I can see that God has been with me throughout all the significant and challenging times—moments of joy or when I was ready to give up. I step into the watch room and look out, amazed at the distance I can see. I immediately recognize how far I have come in life.

Suddenly without warning, the sky darkens, and mighty waves sweep vigorously against the shore surrounding the lighthouse—waves of opposition, betrayal, pain, disappointment, and suffering. But I am not afraid—I am at peace because the lighthouse was built on solid rock with a brilliant light, Jesus, guiding and calming me through all that is treacherous and frightening. Jesus said, "I am the light of the world."

I believe that God's "…word is a lamp to guide my feet and a light for my path" (See Psalm 119:105 NIV). One day I will hear Jesus calling me home—until then I will trust in "the light of the world," who assures me that I am never alone.

If Jesus comes today, I will step into heaven and will be dancing on the streets of gold in a place of eternal bliss. My soul will be at total PEACE—with my "LIGHTHOUSE."

—Sonya Andres

Overwhelmed

At a home group study, the word "overwhelmed" kept whirling around in my mind, and I had no idea why. The following day I was informed at our writers' group meeting that each writer should prayerfully consider a theme word for the year for the upcoming devotional publication.

"Overwhelmed" then became two categories for me: Overwhelmed by Life, and Overwhelmed by God, as at any given time, most of us will find ourselves in one of those categories. I sincerely hope that this collection of devotions will make you smile, think, and pray and that ultimately, you will find yourself overwhelmed by the Wonder that is Jesus.

End-Of-The-Month Food

"Blessed are those who hunger and thirst for
righteousness, for they shall be filled."
Matthew 5:6 (NKJV)

As I pushed the grocery cart through the aisles, I saw an adorable little boy sitting in another cart as his mother tossed in various food items. "What's that?" he asked as she tossed in bags of rice, beans, and lentils. "End-of-the-month food," she said. I giggled and we exchanged glances and grins of understanding. Ah yes, end-of-the-month food: what you stock in the pantry for those times when there is more month than money.

Yes, been there, done that, got more than one *T-shirt*! Financial struggles are not unknown to most of us. Sometimes they exist through no fault of our own, but more often than not, we may find ourselves looking for that "end-of-the-month food" because we have mismanaged or overspent on our selfish desires.

There is no need to feel overwhelmed by your need. I am so very thankful that my God is a provider. He will lead me into paths teaching me obedience and responsibility (such as the discipline of tithing), but He is faithful to His Word also when he tells us in Psalm 37:25 (NKJV), "yet I have not seen the righteous forsaken, nor his descendants begging bread." Or, in Philippians 4:19 (NKJV) where we read, "And my God shall supply all your need according to His riches in glory by Christ Jesus." God is faithful to meet our physical needs.

But there is another type of hunger that our precious Father is also faithful to meet—a sincere longing for HIM! If we hunger after Him, we will be filled.

Come to think of it I am feeling rather hungry right about now!

—Carmen Mosher

Faith

*"Fear not, for I am with you; be not dismayed, for
I am your God. I will strengthen you,
yes, I will help you, I will uphold you with My righteous right hand."*
Isaiah 41:10 (KJV)

I admitted! I am one of those "stupid", crazy in love with my grandkid's kind of grandmother. They can do no wrong—I don't care what their parents say! From the moment I gazed into the face of my first grandson I was certain that this is what I had been born for. At times I have wished I could have just skipped ahead to the grand-parenting and avoided the parenting, but alas, there is an order to these things.

We have been blessed with six grandchildren by birth, and one by heart (some call them step-grandchildren) but they all are unique and cherished. So, I remember the thrill of the phone call informing us that another blessing was on the way. Never mind that the parents had not planned for a child—God has a way of ignoring our plans. In case you haven't noticed—we were excited that they were expecting a new one.

Several weeks later, we were informed that this wonder was another girl, much to my delight, and they had selected her name, Faith Helen. Okay, if I were not already in love with this unseen bundle, I was now because her middle name would be after my wonderful mother. I was thrilled that my son and his wife would honor her memory in this way.

Then, at about halfway through the pregnancy, my dear "daughter-in-heart" lost the baby. We were all devastated. Overwhelmed, I sobbed out my **"Why"** questions to God, thinking I would not receive an answer. My heart would be **forever** knit to a child I would never hold. I would **forever** miss the laughter I would never hear. I would **forever** long for the hugs that would never be given.

Then, overwhelmed by God's love like the dawning of a warm summer day, the real truth began to warm my broken heart. Separation from us did not mean lost to us. Our beautiful baby Faith is snuggled in the arms of her heavenly Father, and one day soon, we will have a grand reunion.

You are so very blessed, my sweet Faith Helen, to walk hand in hand now with our Jesus, and I am pretty sure your great-grandma Helen is walking with you too. I can't wait to take a stroll with you all!

—Carmen Mosher

For Such A Time As This

"...and who knoweth whether thou art come to
the kingdom for such a time as this?"
Esther 4:14 (KJV)

The deadline was approaching like an on-time freight train—and I was not ready. I hadn't been procrastinating, not really. I had been thinking about my assignment a lot, but thinking does not equal action, and now the pressure was mounting with every passing minute.

Have you ever been there? Everyone depended upon you. All eyes looked to you for the needed action and hoped for result. Oy—the pressure!

This kind of stress must have been what poor little Jewish beauty queen Esther felt. In the book of Esther, we read the account of a diabolical plot—orchestrated by the schemer, Haman—to obliterate the Jewish people. The plot thickens as the reigning queen displeases her king, and he dethrones her and seeks a replacement. Esther's beauty places her among the candidates and, yay! She wins the king's heart!

Her wise cousin, Mordecai, tried to focus her thoughts and resolve for the bold move to approach the throne of the king—uninvited—on behalf of her fellow Jews. You see, this was not done, folks! But lest she becomes entirely overwhelmed by the stakes at hand—Mordecai encouraged her with these words -- "For if you remain completely silent at this time, relief and deliverance will arise for the Jews from another place—and who knoweth whether thou art come into the kingdom for such a time as this?" (See Esther 4:14 - KJV.) Ah, cousin Mordecai understood that God was not limited to the action and response of this future queen of Persia.

I find it interesting that God is not named in the book of Esther, but His plan and provision are a constant thread. No doubt He had many options available, but God chose to use the submissive Esther to protect and deliver His people. How dare we ever be so puffed up as to think that we are God's only option? It is an honor for God to choose to include us as a tool in His plan, but we should never think that we are the only tool in the shed!

—Carmen Mosher

"I'm So Sorry, Mrs. Mosher"

"He heals the brokenhearted and binds up their wounds."
Psalm 147:3 (NKJV)

The doctor's words hung in the air like an arrow at its apex before plummeting to its target. "I'm so sorry, Mrs. Mosher. The test results are indicating a condition that will make it nearly impossible for you to conceive." My husband and I had been working on having a baby for quite some time. Well, okay, there was a little fun involved, but more than two years had passed and still we were not pregnant. We had been to numerous medical appointments and tests already and today's news was not welcomed.

Our compassionate fertility specialist was babbling on about next appointment and possible options but his words, "impossible for you to conceive," swirled in my head like water flowing down a drain. Somehow, I managed to walk to the car where my husband gently patted my knee and said, "It will be okay, Honey."

"Okay? How will it be okay?" I blurted out, with tears brimming my eyes like flood waters overwhelming their banks. My greatest hope lay shattered at my feet—my prayers like a forgotten, unopened gift after the party's end.

I tried to imagine our lives without the hugs, giggles, and noise of toddlers. I tried to picture it, but I could not. Quiet tears rolled down my cheeks for the first half of our thirty-mile trip home. Then slowly, like the sun breaking over the horizon, the faith in my heart began to dawn upon the grief in my brain. My God could do anything! He had proved it to me over and over. He had shown it to me through my healing as a little girl.

I smiled gently and spoke my faith to my husband and my God, "You are right Hon, it will be okay. God knows my desire for He has put it in my heart. He created my body, and He is certainly able to heal it. He will give us our child. I may not know how, or even when, but I declare it now and will stand upon it until I see it happen." The tears dried upon my cheeks as peace spread through my heart like butter on hot pancakes. I didn't know how or when, but I felt sure that one day, I would hold a sweet baby in my arms, made possible through the miraculous work of my loving God.

And, P.S. — I did!

—Carmen Mosher

The Empty Freezer

*"But my God shall supply all your need according
to his riches in glory by Christ Jesus."*
Philippians 4:19 (KJV)

I closed the freezer door and set the turkey into the sink of cold water to thaw. My sister and her husband would be arriving soon for the weekend. I sighed and thought, *Well, Lord, I will share such as I have here, and I thank you for your provision, but you know as well as I do that the freezer is now empty.*

Our guests arrived, and we gave them a tour of our parsonage, a little house that sat behind the church where we were serving as associate pastors. As we passed through the kitchen, my sister noticed the turkey thawing in the sink and said, "Oh Carm, you didn't need to go to the trouble of a turkey dinner just for us!" I gave a nervous little laugh, wondering if I should share the whole truth with her.

"Oh, it's no trouble at all, you are worth it...Besides, that bird was my only option!"

True to her compassionate nature, she inquired if we were doing okay (meaning—do you guys need money?) We received a meager salary in addition to our housing provision but had two children and just as many bills as the next guy. Of course, we needed money! But I was determined not to dump my problems on her and replied that we were okay. After all, God had called us to serve this little church. We were His concern, and I am quite sure that He was not feeling overwhelmed at the thought of my empty freezer.

We were enjoying catching up when suddenly there was a knock on my back door. I shot my sister a puzzled look and went to the door. There stood a young woman from our church with several grocery bags at her feet. "Hey Carmen, sorry to not call first, but we just butchered a cow, and our freezer is overflowing. I hope you guys can use this meat." She helped me put the wrapped treasure into the freezer, kindly not mentioning its lack of contents. I voiced appreciation over and over for their generosity until she told me just to shut up!

Later that weekend as we feasted on roast turkey and mashed potatoes, we lingered around the table discussing the goodness of God. We may think that He has missed some great opportunities to be early, but He is never late." The Lord knew our need and then filled our freezer. There would be many more times in the years to come when circumstances would threaten to overwhelm us. God proved to me that weekend that He cares about our needs and has taken care of every detail.

Do you have an empty freezer? No problem for Jehovah Jireh!

—Carmen Mosher

The Great Composer

"And he hath put a new song in my mouth, even praise unto our God: many shall see it, and fear, and shall trust in the Lord."
Psalm 40:3 (KJV)

We had taken the mission assignment with excitement and anticipation. Years earlier we had received a prophetic word that we would preach overseas. We felt that our proposed two years in Kingston, Jamaica, was the fulfillment of that prophesy.

After a year and a half of working with limited tools to establish the new church, we were unexpectedly informed that we would not return as associate pastors. We were devastated. We had served faithfully for three years before coming to Jamaica. We sacrificed family and given up much to move to a church where we knew no one. And, we did it all again when we moved to Jamaica. We served to expect that our church would send someone to continue the mission work, and we would return to serve in a congregation, which we had grown to love. But now we found ourselves jobless, homeless, possession-less, and yes, nearly overwhelmed by hopelessness. It was not our plan.

In hindsight, we saw that our devastation was His orchestration because shortly, we were offered a staff position in a ministry outreach of a church in California. We would be ministering with dear friends whom we had prayed and dreamed of working with for years.

Little did we realize that God was composing a grand symphony of our lives. From the prelude, that was His calling, through the final curtain call that will be our heavenly entrance. He is writing every note. The melody may not always be of our choosing, but what we do not see, what we do not know, is that He has already sung over us a beautiful and often complicated melody. I will return a new song of praise to Him, confident that the final note will bring down the house!

Don't be overwhelmed—Sing a new song!

—Carmen Mosher

When You Come to The End of Yourself

"Wherefore take unto you the whole armour of God, that ye may be able to withstand in the evil day, and having done all, to stand."
Ephesians 6:13 (KJV)

"I don't know what else to do. I've tried everything I can think of. I've got nothing left to give."

Why do we insist on fighting every battle in our flesh first? It is when we have exhausted our strength, ideas, and resources that the light dawns upon us that, just perhaps, God might be able to assist.

The moment we align ourselves with the King and His Kingdom, we become an enemy of the evil one. Satan's goal is summed up—to steal, kill, and destroy. Why are we surprised when the attacks come? And how stupid (yes, I said stupid) is it to try to fight on a spiritual plane with human weapons and wisdom?

When we come to the end of ourselves, acknowledging that we are frail and weak, defenseless and clueless, then, and only then, are we stripped down to our skivvies and ready to put on the armor already provided. *We armor up* to protect against an enemy, who God is fighting, and will ultimately defeat.

The Apostle Paul of the New Testament lists in detail the components of our armor and what each item will do for us. He also states in the Scripture above, "Put on the whole armor of God!" Having it polished and sitting in your closet will not be much help when the battles begin. We are given a straightforward instruction—**TO STAND**.

So, when you feel overwhelmed, stop running around in your underwear and get on that glorious armor!

—Carmen Mosher

...OVERWHELMED BY LIFE—
BE OVERWHELMED BY GOD

Blinded by The Light

*"And as he [Saul of Tarsus] journeyed, he came near Damascus: and suddenly
there shined round about him a light from heaven"*
Acts 9:3 (KJV)

Ah, Saul! Educated! Prideful! Passionate! Driven (albeit in the wrong direction)! On his way to Damascus to harass those crazy Christians! Cue the "Blinding Light!"

Look at what Jesus says to him, "It is hard for you to kick against the goads." A goad was a sharp, pointed stick used to urge oxen to move forward and to follow the desired path. Ha! I love the symbolism of Scripture! Saul then is depicted as a rather slow, methodical beast that has been stuck a few times to urge him in the right direction. Do you think that the testimonies of the many people Saul had persecuted and imprisoned had not been prickling at his educated, logical brain? But he was so determined to stay his course, pride intact, that all those jabs had not turned him onto a different path but had indeed left a mark or two.

At least, the next thing out of his mouth was an improvement. It was not until Saul, blinded by the light of heaven and hearing the voice of God, asked, "Lord, what do you want me to do?" What followed is one of the most overwhelming conversion experiences ever recorded. Direction, focus, passion, and heart forever changed. The name change was just a bonus! As a result of his dramatic conversion, his name was changed to Paul.

One way or another, we will be changed when we come face to face with the reality of the Savior. Ours may not be as dramatic as Paul's, but we will be changed—miraculously, gloriously changed, and set on a new path that leads to a forever with "Our Blinding Light!"

—Carmen Mosher

Boy, Oh Boy

"...take now your son, your only son Isaac, whom you love,
and go to the land of Moriah, and offer him there as a burnt
offering on one of the mountains of which I shall tell you."
Genesis 22:2 (NKJV)

I'm sure you have received a birth announcement or baby shower invitation in the mail and rejoiced with those new parents on the arrival of their squishy new bundle of joy. So, I am sure you can imagine the overwhelming delight of Old Testament saints, Abraham and Sarah, when their long promised and hoped for son, Isaac, makes his entrance into the genealogy line of Scripture.

Let's fast forward a dozen or so years. Abraham finds himself hiking up a mountain with his beloved Isaac to sacrifice unto the Lord. But wait—they have everything they need, except the sacrifice. Can you imagine Abraham's thoughts as he planted one foot in front of the other for three days trying his best to climb as slowly as possible without raising suspicions in Isaac? Was he mentally writing the eulogy for his young son? Was he recounting the promise made, the years waiting, the miraculous pregnancy, the unparalleled joy upon the birth of their son, the years of sheer joy and laughter he had brought into their golden years? Was he trying to prepare for the task assigned to him mentally? Was he thinking about how he would explain all this to Sarah?

Was Abraham thinking on these things as he hiked, or with each footfall was he screaming in his heart—but God you promised? God seldom reveals His purpose to us as He unveils His plan. But there is always a purpose in His plan, and it is usually bigger than we could imagine and more far-reaching than we could dream.

God promised to give a boy, and He delivered. Then He required that boy as a sacrifice to be offered by his father. Then he spared that boy and provided a substitutionary sacrifice in the ram. Again, God delivered. No matter the challenge you might be facing, I can assure you that He will deliver—boy, oh boy, will He deliver!

—Carmen Mosher

Burn, Baby Burn

*"And the angel of the Lord appeared unto him in a
flame of fire out of the midst of a bush: and he
looked, and behold, the bush burned with fire,
and the bush was not consumed."*
Exodus 3:2 (KJV)

"Okay folks, so me and the flock were just hanging out in the desert the other day when I see this bush that is burning; only it is no ordinary bush and no ordinary fire." Ya' think?

So, begins the story of which epic movies are made. Seriously! Have you noticed that when God gives an assignment, He prefaces it with an amazing announcement? Well, a fire-talking bush is pretty amazing.

Most Bible scholars understand that the Angel of the Lord, who spoke to Moses of the Old Testament from the burning bush was the pre-incarnate Jesus Christ. They also attribute the fire that did not consume the bush as the Shekinah glory of God. Moses' task was to deliver the Israelites from bondage—that by man's standards was impossible. Moses presents his list of excuses which God systematically dismisses. But then, who can argue with the Son of God surrounded by His glory?

I am pretty sure that Moses felt overwhelmed by the magnitude of the task assigned to him. He would experience step by step, day by day, the power of the God of his ancestors, who would accomplish exactly what He said He would do. The Moses, who ran away from Egypt, was not the Moses who returned. The Moses, who returned had a life-changing encounter, with God and the Moses, who left Egypt a second time, leading an entire nation to their deliverance, had been transformed by the Shekinah glory of God. The glory of God will indeed change us, overwhelm us, and forever shine brightly through our testimony.

—Carmen Mosher

Dream Weaver

*"And he said unto them, Hear, I pray you, this dream
which I have dreamed: for behold, we were
binding sheaves in the field, and lo, my sheaf arose,
and also stood upright; and, behold, your
sheaves stood round about, and made obeisance to my sheaf."*
Genesis 37:6-7 (KJV)

I love Joseph of the Old Testament. Is this man not overwhelmingly amazing? Starting out as a teenager with bullies for brothers, he failed to exercise discernment over enthusiasm, as God gives him a couple of rather incredible dream promises. The favorite child of his father, Jacob, made evident by that vivid coat he loved to wear (some scholars believe this coat, signifying the preferred child status, was made and intricately embroidered by his mother, Rachel.) Acting on their jealousy, his brothers threw poor, preferred little Joseph into a dried up well. And, his troubles are only beginning!

What I find so amazing about Joseph is that even though there is a pretty significant gap of time between his brothers' betrayal and Joseph's rise to power in Egypt, not one word of complaint is recorded as having proceeded from his lips! If written on tiny slips of paper, my grumblings would have more than filled up that stupid well!

Joseph's faith in his dream promise stood firm throughout his slavery, false accusations, and imprisonment. He remained humble through his rise to power, confident that God would bring every detail of his dreams into fulfillment. What amazing faith! What insight into the hand of God upon his life! Just as impressive is his genuine love for his brothers upon their reunion, affirming to them that God's plan, birthed through a teenager's dreams so long ago, was for the salvation of His people.

Oh, that we might, in some small measure, be able to learn the lessons for the same unwavering faith that Joseph's life displayed.

—Carmen Mosher

I'm Not Letting Go

*"Then Jacob was left alone; and there wrestled a man
with him until the breaking of the day."*
Genesis 32:24 (KJV)

Can you just imagine the announcer for the Old Testament wrestling match introducing the participants? "Now, we have in this corner the title holder—The One and only Angel of the Lord, also known as the pre-incarnate Jesus Christ, the Messiah. And, in the opposing corner Jacob, the schemer, also known as the supplanter, and known to his brother as "little heel grabber." This fight will be for one very long round—'until the breaking of the day.' Alright gentlemen, let the match begin."

And so, begins the most significant sporting contest ever witnessed by heaven. We know that God is omniscient, and nothing surprises Him, but I, for one, was somewhat surprised and impressed by the tenacity of Jacob.

Jacob led a roller coaster life—tricking and tricked by, and at long last making his way back home, dreading every step that brought him closer to the imminent reunion with Esau, the brother whose birthright and blessing he stole.

The scriptural account of this event does not indicate that the match was all one-sided. We know that Jacob stubbornly held on, refusing to let go of his heavenly opponent. It says that when "He" (the Angel) saw that He did not prevail against him (Jacob), He touched the socket of his hip and Jacob continued to wrestle with his hip out of joint! Now, that is one stubborn man determined not to leave until he received the blessing.

It had taken nearly a lifetime to realize, but dear ol' Jacob was tired of his scheming ways. He, at last, wanted to get it right, and God rewarded him with a blessing and a new name. Jacob, the schemer, is transformed into Israel, the fighter.

I think that a new name, a blessing from God, and a chance to turn his life around probably made the limp he walked away with a little easier to accept. And like most of us, a constant overwhelming reminder that character adjustment isn't a bad idea either.

—Carmen Mosher

Overshadowed

"And the angel answered and said unto her, The Holy Ghost
shall come upon thee, and the power of the Highest shall overshadow thee;
therefore also that holy thing which shall be born
of thee shall be called the Son of God."
Luke 1:35 (KJV)

Book by book of the Bible, chapter by chapter, God provided clues to His chosen people regarding the Messiah. He hinted at and revealed bits of information over hundreds of years as to the timing and identity of the Savior King, who would come. But His arrival looked nothing like the Jewish nation had anticipated!

An ordinary young girl named Mary had an extraordinary encounter with an angelic being named Gabriel, with an even more remarkable message: "You will conceive in your womb and bring forth a son and shall call His name Jesus." Now I remember the excitement I felt upon being informed I was pregnant the first time; but then, I was already married! Not so with young Mary. Engaged but not yet married, she was a virgin, so she thought this visitor and his announcement to be a bit "out there." I suspect that as Gabriel shared more details, Mary's mind whirled as the truth washed over her. The awe, the wonder, the questions, no doubt followed by sheer terror!

To be unwed and pregnant barely carries any negative consequence in our society today, even within the church, but not so in Mary's day. Her life was on the line as the punishment for adultery was to be stoned to death. And no one, probably even Joseph, her betrothed, would believe that the mysterious Gabriel had spoken these wonders to her. I am sure that Mary felt more than a bit overwhelmed by it all.

The time that elapsed between Gabriel's announcement and the evidence of her pregnancy is not told in Scripture, but Mary received the news with an humble spirit and rejoicing heart.

Precious, young, submissive Mary was overwhelmed by unusual, life-changing events. She progresses from being overwhelmed by life to being overwhelmed by God.

Dear Mary: you and I have that last bit in common.

—Carmen Mosher

Strength In Hiding

"And the angel of the Lord appeared unto him, and said unto him,
the Lord is with thee, thou mighty man of valour."
Judges 6:12 (KJV)

I have always chuckled when I read this introduction to Gideon of the Bible. There he is—hiding out in the winepress, threshing out grain for his family's survival, hoping the Midianites won't find him. Then, the Angel of the Lord appears, and Gideon seems to be a bit confused— "The Lord is with you, you mighty man of valor!" Really? Do you not see the overwhelmed man who is hiding? What kind of valor is that?

But God sees us as we can be, not as we are. God knew that Gideon needed a little push, okay, a rather big shove, in the right direction. God calls us as He sees us, not as we see ourselves. He sees our potential, not our weakness. We see the assignment given as overwhelming, not able to see ahead that His answer is even bigger. We see our faith as microscopic, while He sees it as a seed about to bring forth an abundant harvest.

Gideon places not one, but two fleeces before the Lord to bolster his faith for the assigned attack against the enemy. Have you ever noticed that God did not fault him for this or see it as a sign of weakness? Gideon asked two questions, which are followed by two distinct answers. Like a faith booster shot.

My friend Gideon, after a couple of faith injections, fulfills his overwhelming assignment and makes it into the Hall of Faith in Hebrews chapter 11.

Don't you just love a happy ending? How will yours read?

—Carmen Mosher

Encouragement

My life story is a testimony to God's power in my life. For decades I thought I was worthless. I lived in a black box of self-condemnation. But God **encouraged** me—in baby steps. Through the years, strangers told me to tell others about my journey.

I pray that by revealing my story, others like me will be **encouraged** to walk with faith and obedience accomplishing God's preordained plan for their lives—never giving up.

So, my word is **"Encouragement."**

Cinderella Girl

*"You intended to harm me, but God intended it for good to
accomplish what is now being done, the saving of many lives."*
Genesis 50:20 (NIV)

I was a middle child. When I was eight, I went outside and looked up at
our house and asked myself this burning question, *did my parents love me?*
I decided that since I had a home, clothes and ate daily; *perhaps, they did
love me?* My father was a tough authoritarian, and my mother was a silent,
introverted person. They never encouraged or praised me, leaving me unable
to believe I was okay. Living in the shadows of my siblings caused me to
become unable to speak up for myself. My sister was four years older and
seemed to be the favorite of my step-grandmother, Anna.

Silently, I called Anna the "witch of Mammoth Street." She was nasty and
never had a kind word for me. I felt that my sister treated me unkindly. She
was "Queen at grandma's house." She was given money, dolls, and clothes, but
Grandma Anna gave me nothing. I was like "Cinderella."

My father died when I was ten. Grandpa Sam was the only one to show
me, love. After Anna died, when I was twelve, I took care of Grandpa; I was
fourteen years old when he died. The wounds of childhood ripped apart
my self-esteem. I believed I would never achieve or be anything, and I felt
blackened by the soot of life—a hapless child with no future.

Be encouraged. God had a plan for me even then. Oddly, my mother, who
I do not believe was a Christian, purchased a Picture Bible Story Book to read
to us, children, at night when we were young. This book put a burning desire
for me to know I was going to heaven when I died. I know that God was behind
that purchase! My mother also made us say a prayer every evening:

"Now I lay me down to sleep I pray the Lord my soul to keep.
If I die before I wake, I pray the Lord, **my soul,** to take."

So—at the age of four from that book and prayer—I knew with all my
little broken being, I wanted to go to heaven when I died. Praise God that my
mother did this. It was not until many years later that God began to heal me.

—Millie Wasden

The Quest

"The steps of a man are established by the LORD, And He delights in his way."
Psalm 37:23 (NASB)

As a young child I was always concerned about going to heaven, but I didn't know how. So as early as I can remember, I was on a quest to find out the truth about going to heaven. Even then, I knew I was a sinner and that my brownie points would not get me to heaven. As I look back now, I see the Holy Spirit was directing my path.

My assigned chores were to dust and polish the furniture—this led me to the bookcase. On the bookshelf, I noticed that only one book claimed to be holy. So, I decided to find my answers in that book—the Bible. I decided to start reading in the New Testament but found it confusing since I was only seven years old.

At the age of twelve, I had to fill out a form stating my religious beliefs—I didn't know what to check. A few years later, my mother left a Bible on the table. I picked it up, and there at the back was the plan of salvation. I signed it.

Years passed; I grew up. I wondered if all there was to life was getting up, going to work, and coming home. What a daily drudge it all was!

When a neighbor invited me to church, I refused to go. However, she was very persistent. Finally, I went. On the way home from church she asked me, "Do you know if you died tonight that you would go to heaven?" I answered, "*I* am not sure."

She explained that going to heaven was a gift of God's grace to those who repent of their sins and have faith to believe that His son, Jesus Christ, died for our sins and was resurrected. That day I finished my quest and received Jesus as my Lord and Savior.

God used all the experiences of a little child to lay the foundation for accepting Him as a young woman. I found meaning and purpose in daily living by trusting God that day.

Isn't that encouraging!

—Millie Wasden

First Baby Step

"Now to him who is able to do immeasurably more than all we ask or imagine, according to his power that is at work within us, to him be glory in the church and in Christ Jesus throughout all generations, for ever and ever! Amen."
Ephesians 3:20 (NIV)

I was twenty-eight years old, married, and raising two children. I had accepted Christ at the young age of twenty. Sadly, I was trapped still in the black box of my mind with low self-esteem, anxiety, and depression—my constant companions. I used to go over to a neighbor's house and complain about my problems. One day, this patient and long-suffering soul suggested that I should do something—like volunteering at the PTA—perhaps that would help. I was terrified! I prayed to the Lord, asking Him what I should do. God convicted me that I should try—even though I believed in my heart, I had nothing to offer. I volunteered for the hospitality section of the PTA. To my horror, the leader of hospitality left within two months. So, not wanting to quit, I assumed that "huge" responsibility of leadership. I decided that I would use tablecloths and decorate the tables with a little bouquet of fresh flowers, just like I did at home. Everyone was complimentary. Like a child, I beamed with amazement and thought *I did this—wow*! Imagine my overflowing joy.

God used my neighbor to get me to take a baby step, to act on my own. God had shown me that I could finally achieve something that was of value to others! My first baby step!

The moral of this story is when tackling any problematic task that God has asked of us—pray. God is our enabler to step out in faith and obedience. God will accomplish his purposes through you, just like he did for Moses, who thought he could not speak effectively to lead God's people (See Exodus 7:1, 2 - NIV) God provided his brother, Aaron, as a speaker for the people. God knew my need to overcome my esteem issues. I believe God purposely had the leader quit so I would go beyond my comfort level. That was the way—He would accomplish how he wanted me to grow and be able to serve him. And, I learned by stepping out, that hospitality is one of the gifts God gave me.

—Millie Wasden

Needy Me

*"Trust in the Lord with all your heart and lean not on
your own understanding; in all your ways submit to
him, and he will make your paths straight."*
Proverbs 3:5,6 (NIV)

Have you ever wondered if a person disliked you? Many years ago, I felt that way. My "person" was the secretary of my children's grammar school. I was a volunteer for the PTA. It seemed to me that she did not like me because she would never smile or talk to me, although she did answer my questions politely. I had seen her react to others with a more encouraging attitude, or so I thought. I needed some encouragement from her, as well. I was feeling rejected and sad. I am sure that I prayed about the situation. One day I walked into her office and received the usual polite answers to my questions. I walked out the door. I could not take it anymore. I decided to take the issue head-on. With all the courage I could muster I went back in and said, "Do you like me?" I was nearly crying. I am sure she was surprised!

With pure sweetness, she said, "Yes, why do you feel that way?" I explained that whenever I come into the office, she never smiled or talked to me but treated me in a businesslike manner. She said, "I am a bit surprised at what you asked, but Millie, I do like you." She apologized so kindly to me.

I was embarrassed, but I learned a terrific lesson; I learned that God knew my problem. He knew how needy I was. I so wanted people to like me.

I learned to be transparent; it freed me from assuming most people didn't like me. Now, I realize the importance of encouraging others. I do not judge a person because of any questions they might ask me. I try to have an open mind. Only the Lord knows each person's heart. The biggest lesson I learned was to trust and lean on the Lord.

—Millie Wasden

In the Pit

*"I am convinced and confident of this very thing, that He who has
begun a good work in you will [continue to] perfect and
complete it until the day of Christ Jesus [the time of His return]."*
Philippians 1:6 (AMP)

For most of my life, even in childhood, I was depressed; it lasted for 45 years during the raising of my children and through my church ministry school volunteering. I had little energy for these important tasks. My life was a pit of depression that affected everything I did and challenged me daily. Sometimes I could not even get out of bed. It made even the holidays a struggle.

One year I suffered a severe breakdown because of my dependence on a friend, who for their good stopped seeing me. I had become a real burden to them with my needy ways. I became so depressed that the nursery school where I worked had to let me go because the parents did not want their children around such a forlorn person. A friend of mine suggested I apply for a job of cleaning her boss' house. They hired me.

I sensed God urging me to listen to Christian programs on the radio, but I refused. While driving to my new job—feeling hopeless, as if I was at the bottom of the pit—God prompted me again—*turn on the radio*. This time I obeyed. Dr. Lloyd John Ogilvie was preaching and for the first time, I felt a ray of hope. I don't remember what he said, but I was so encouraged.

I bought a radio and listened every day while doing my housework. Sometimes, God would use the preachers to bring me to my knees and pray—this was a time of growth, and I started to heal. It was a moment-by-moment time with God. Some years later, in my healing process, I needed to go to Hollywood Presbyterian Church, where Dr. Ogilvie was speaking. I had the opportunity to tell him how much his sermon had encouraged me. I will never forget how he in sheer amazement, threw back his head and, to my surprise, said he loved my story and wanted to put it into his next newsletter.

I realized I was codependent and needy and drove my friends away. Knowing that I had such a problem encouraged me to accept myself and look for help. Praise God for the revelation.

—Millie Wasden

God Uses Us Anyway

*"...He said to me 'My grace is sufficient for you, for
my power is made perfect in weakness.'"*
2 Corinthians 12:9 (NIV)

During my life I have learned a very important lesson that has encouraged me. I pray that this lesson will also encourage others, who have suffered from depression or other adversities—God uses us where we are, even when we are suffering.

My deep desire was to be an actress or model, but something held me back from doing it—perhaps the lifestyle? However, God fulfilled this desire through other gifts.

Even though I was often afraid or uncomfortable, I stepped out in faith. God showed me I had talents, and He often fulfilled my desires through Christian means. In my career as a dental assistant, God revealed that I had a knack for working with people. Later, I modeled in many fashions shows at fundraising events for a Christian Women's Club and served as moderator at large functions—this met my desire for modeling and speaking in front of others.

Christian counseling helped me learn that God loved me just as I was. Today, I have more clarity about who I am and what God has for me. I am still a little insecure, but I know I am valued, and I have peace.

When God gives you a gift, serve Him in obedience, and meet the needs of others, and He will fill your deepest needs and desires.

**"Our infirmities become the black velvet on which the
diamond of God's love glitters all the more brightly."**
Charles Spurgeon (1863)

—Millie Wasden

Black Legs

"A cheerful heart is good medicine,.."
Proverbs 17:22 (NIV)

Sometimes odd things happen for Godly reasons! Several years ago, I bought a lovely outfit to wear for my 50th school reunion. The jacket was turquoise and black. Recently, I decided to wear this jacket for church together with flowing black pants. Usually, I wore it for a few hours, but this day was different. After going to church, I met a client and then went shopping. Returning home many hours later, I glanced down and noticed some odd-looking marks on my foot, ankle, and lower leg. Later that night, when I finally decided to change outfits, I noticed that my legs were black! That startled me. A close friend had just suffered a blood clot, and her leg had turned black, so I decided to go to the emergency room.

My vitals were excellent, and the doctor was pleased but perplexed about the color of my legs. He had never seen anything quite like this! In trying to figure out the problem, the nurse asked what I had been wearing that day. I told her about the black pants. She came with a washcloth and applied it to my legs. To our surprise, the color came off! I felt a little foolish, but the nurse had a good laugh and said, "We needed some comic relief here since there has been a big accident and several ambulances are on their way here now." It's encouraging to know that the Bible says, "A cheerful heart is good medicine."

On my journey home, several ambulances passed us on their way to the hospital—sirens and lights flashing. I believe God set these events in motion so I could pray for the people involved in the accident.

—Millie Wasden

"IF YOU'RE FEELING HELPLESS,
HELP SOMEONE."
Aung San Suu Kyi

Listening to God

*"Many are the plans in a person's heart, but it is
the Lord's purposes that prevails."*
Proverbs 19:21 (NIV)

We all have projects we have to do in a timely manner. I had a deadline for my writers' group. I had the responsibility to write fourteen devotions! I had three of them close to being finished, some minor changes on a few, and had to still write one more. I thought I had loads of time, so I put off getting them done. Daily, God prompted me to sit down and complete the changes and write the other devotions.

I wanted to start my own business back up. My thoughts were more on my business, but there was a positive spirit from God not to proceed with this. I was obedient and did not start my business back up. Praise God! I still put off the writing.

We need to listen and act on His leading and know when He has our best in mind. He did have something better for my future to bless me.

A few weeks later, my brother called. He said he had an echocardiogram and they found some serious heart issues. He asked if I could come to be with him. He needed support and encouragement—his wife died two years before. He children could not help him. We had not seen each other in the last 50 years, so this gave us time to get to know each other again.

When he was feeling better, I asked if we could go to church? It was the first time in many years he was able to go. After church, he was encouraged to have found support in the people who attended.

Praise God! He used this circumstance to bless my brother and me. Before our meals, we would say grace, and he learned to trust God. His prayers were so sweet. He gave God his daily and future needs concerning his heart.

Through God, I was able to encourage my brother and watch our relationship grow—now I am off to work on writing my devotions.

—Millie Wasden

Encouraged

"But those who wait for the Lord [who expect, look for,
and hope in Him] Will gain new strength and
renew their power; They will lift up their wings [and rise
up close to God] like eagles [rising toward the
sun]; They will run and not become weary, They will walk and not grow tired."
Isaiah 40:31 (AMP)

In the spring of 2015, my daughter notified me that they had to move from their home of 9 years. They had two months to find a place in San Jose, California. After looking, they realized that they couldn't afford to live there. A salary increase for her husband was not possible. Instead, his employer suggested transferring to Atlanta, Georgia. God provided them all they needed to make the move—what a miracle!

Moving from San Jose, however, left them drowning in debt. My daughter prayed and asked God for wisdom. Through a debt settlement company, they were able to pay down their debt and save money for their first house. Then in January of 2018, Mark, her husband, was told he was going to be laid off after 17 years; with only one and one-half months of severance pay. Then the rental agency notified them they were raising their rent, and they had to move or renegotiate their lease. Mark went to many interviews. There was nothing. My daughter was terrified; I asked *how I could pray for them.* She explained he wasn't qualified for the more modern technology that most jobs require.

God showed me that I needed to pray, specifically. I asked my church friends and other people to pray for what Mark needed. That is just what happened! He got a new job.

Her heart and mind were sustained and given encouragement through answered prayer and clinging to God's Word.

—Millie Wasden

Answered Prayer

"Do not merely listen to the word, and so deceive yourselves. Do what it says."
James 1:22 (NIV)

Four years ago, I needed a complete knee replacement. I heard that it was a difficult operation with a painful and long recovery. The orthopedic doctor described the procedure in very graphic terms. I was horrified and very frightened of the operation. I decided not to use that doctor. I prayed a great deal about the situation. God prompted me to ask an odd question at a routine appointment with my pain management doctor, who I really trusted. "Doctor, I have decided to put all my eggs in one basket!"

He asked me, "What do you mean?"

I explained how frightened I was of the knee operation and that I wanted him to do it. He told me very gently that he only did pain management but that he wanted me to take care of my knee. He suggested a doctor at the University of Arizona. This orthopedic doctor turned out to be excellent and calmed all my fears. His personality, bedside manner, and skill were the best. I had only one concern I wanted the best anesthesiologist. The selected anesthesiologist indicated that a spinal block rather than anesthetic would be the best option for a speedier recovery.

The big day arrived. When the nurse tried to get the IV started, it would not work. She was going to get help when I said, "Wait, calm down—let me pray for you and then try again." She waited, and I prayed to help her start the IV. She tried again, and it ran like a river! Praise God!

Then, I went into the operating room where the anesthesiologist attempted with no success to give me a spinal block. Frustrated, she said, "It is not taking."

At that moment, I encouraged her to stop and let me pray. In front of all the operating room doctors and nurses, I did just that—a witness to His power and might. She tried again, and on the second try, it took—a light to His wonderful and powerful care for me that day! After I came out of the operating room, my nurse commented she had seldom seen such an aware and lucid patient after such complicated surgery.

Isn't it encouraging to know God answers prayer?

—Millie Wasden

Surviving Abuse

"O My God, I trust, lean on, rely on, and am confident in You.
Let me not be put to shame or [my hope in You] be disappointed;
let not my enemies triumph over me."
Psalm 25:2 (AMPC)

At the age of six, I attended a Sunday School class for first and second graders. An older man was assigned to help direct those children, who arrived late to get to their correct classroom. He was always very nice and polite to the adults, and he took a special interest in me every time I was late. He said to me, "You are a bad girl for being late," in a harsh whisper, while forcibly holding me on his knee. He not only did that to scare me, but he also touched me inappropriately. I was a shy little girl and when I tried to let people know they wouldn't listen to me.

Individual family members have also been abusive to me throughout my childhood and into young adulthood. I have painful memories of having to hide under my bed as a child—shaking and crying in absolute terror. It has taken me thirty-five years to figure out that these things which have happened to me are real memories and not just a recurring nightmare.

Abuse leaves you feeling unworthy to be loved and that there must be something wrong with you. But *BE ENCOURAGED*—seeking God through prayer can heal you from the inside out. I don't know why this happened to me, but through my experiences, I want to help others understand that God loves them and made them for a purpose. He will not only help you to cultivate healthy and loving friendships, but He will even give you the ability to forgive those who have harmed you. He has also shown me how much He loves me and has taught me to love myself. God has provided me with a loving and understanding husband to share my life.

"O Lord God, I cried to You for help, and You have healed me."
Psalm 30:2 (AMPC)

—Kristine Richardson

Joy In Your Circumstances

"Consider it pure joy, my brothers and sisters,
whenever you face trials of many kinds,"
James 1:2 (NIV)

During the last fourteen years I have learned some hard lessons about being joyful in circumstances. They are to pray, keep in the Word, trust and be obedient to God, seek Godly advice, be grateful and good stewards of what God has given you, and use your life to bless others with what you have to glorify God.

To illustrate these principles, I would like to tell you the story about my beautiful home. In 2000 we bought our house. I thought it was too lovely to be owned by a person like me. I did not deserve it. In the first years of ownership, I was so busy playing Christian to meet my own emotional needs—not being in the Word or praying like I should (as I understand now)—I was spiritually vulnerable. Then, fourteen years ago, something went wrong. We nearly lost our home!

We made some bad choices regarding money. The situation deteriorated to the point where we received a notice of foreclosure. I panicked! One night I was awakened by God and found that I had been praying in my sleep. I felt God saying to me, Millie, you are in fear, and that is a sin! You are not trusting me. He reminded me to confess my sin of worrying (See 1 John 1:9.)

Instantly, I acknowledged this truth and asked for His forgiveness and peace. God gave me peace and joy. I still had concerns over saving our home, but I trusted everything would work out—although I could not see how He would do it. God provided the means to pay the back payments required, and we were able to get a more affordable loan. God gave me the ability to forgive and trust Him.

God has always taken care of our needs. We have never missed a meal and always paid our bills. I believe that God permitted the near loss of our home to show others that one can go through something tragic, and God will still work it for good. We must be good stewards of what He has given us and share it with others—to share our home for God's glory, not our own.

I am so encouraged and thank God daily, that He reminded me
He takes care of our needs.

—Millie Wasden

God's Protection

*"The steps of a good man are ordered by the LORD: and
he delighteth in his way."*
Psalm 37:23 (KJV)

As a family we have often taken vacations, camping in our RV. Usually these have gone well except on this one occasion. We were returning from a family reunion in Iowa in our RV. We had planned to stop in a certain town in Nebraska. On our way there, my daughter and I both noticed a campground listed in our RV camping guide that offered some fun amenities—horseback riding, hayrides, cookouts, and a very beautiful setting, but we thought no more about it.

Having traveled a long distance, we stopped to get gas and got out to shop. Immediately, my daughter and I caught sight of a flier advertising the same campground we had noticed in our camping guide. Even though our original idea was to go further, we decided to stop in the attractively advertised campsite for family fun for a few days. God had other plans for us.

The skies were somewhat cloudy and the more we traveled to the campsite the fiercer and more foreboding the skies became. As we went in to register, the storm struck with lightning and hail. We were stranded inside with no electricity. By the time the power came back on, we were encouraged by the fantastic news—the main storm hit with the full force of a destructive tornado in the little town in which we had planned to stay.

We were so grateful that God's hand had protected and kept us safe through it all.

—Millie Wasden

Showing Forth God's Power

*"Now to him who is able to do immeasurably more than all we ask
or imagine, according to his power that is at work within us,"*
Ephesians 3:20 (NIV)

God often brings challenges into our lives to grow us and to use for His glory.

From time to time, I discussed with my neighbor that, in my estimation, I was unable to do anything. She asked me, "Can you cook?"

Learning that I could cook, she suggested that I volunteer for the PTA at our local grammar school. I decided that I could do that if I was not "in charge." However, God had different plans—I had the lead position for two years. I also started taking notes for meetings. Since I am dyslectic and unable to spell, God enabled me to do this.

My next roll was Chairman of the Ways and Means Committee. This involved fundraisers for the school, including candy drives and the huge Fall Festival. During my years of working in this position, the others saw something in me that I didn't realize—they saw my faith in action and God in me—even though I was feeling very inadequate and fearful inside.

One Fall Festival I planned for a circus to come. Unfortunately, it rained the night before, and when I arrived the next morning, the President of the PTA said, "Millie, I know you have a way with God. Will you please pray that the projected rain stays at the other end of the valley, so we don't have to cancel the festival?"

God heard my prayer. It did not rain, and we had a successful Fall Festival. It was all for God's glory and my growth and increasing confidence. Had I given up, instead of trusting God in faith and obedience, people would not have seen God's power working in me. Finally, I am encouraged that my deepest dream of today was fulfilled—to be a witness to you, the reader, of what God's power flowing through an obedient person can achieve.

—Millie Wasden

Quiet

In the fall of 2016, my writers' group decided to ask God to give each writer a word to be used in composing devotions after prayer, meditation, and study. When we received the assignment, I was confident I would receive mine quickly. I tried several words, but none seem to be the right one. Christmas came and went, and I began to panic! I didn't have one, and the deadline was in January!

No need to fear, God is always on time. He gave me my word while my husband and I were in Florida on vacation. We were traveling to the Holy Land Experience, when the word "quiet," repeatedly used in a radio sermon, resonated with my spirit. Nevertheless, I wondered why God had given me, what I thought was, an "odd" word. I believed He would have given me something more spiritual—faith, hope, love, etc. That was not His plan. "Quiet" was my word!

"Quiet" in the Greek means, properly still, i.e., steady (settled) due to a divinely inspired inner calmness. It also describes being "appropriately tranquil" by not misusing (or overusing) words that would stir up needless friction (destructive commotion.)

For two years, God took me on an incredible journey of experiencing and understanding "quiet" in my life—that divinely-inspired inner calmness, that is only available from Jesus Christ and His promise to never leave or forsake me. And, now I want to share what I learned with you.

Adoption Day

*"God decided in advance to adopt us into his own family by bringing
us to himself through Jesus Christ. This is what he wanted to do,
and it gave him great pleasure."*
Ephesians 1:5 (NLT)

There were no drum rolls, marching bands, paparazzi, or fancy parties in my honor on my adoption day—that amazing day Jesus became my Lord and Savior. There was only the "quiet" presence of the Holy Spirit assuring me that I was now truly a child of the King. In the depths of my soul, He subtly impressed that I had begun a life-long journey to my eternal home in heaven—a bright new beginning for me with my sins forgiven and His calming and nurturing existence resident in my soul.

I learned that with adoption come privileges—all the promises and blessings of God, carefully delineated in the Bible. There are also admonitions to make my journey calmer, more pleasant. However, if I make mistakes or stray along the way, which I have and will invariably do, it is strongly advised that I confess those errors, those sins, and ask God's forgiveness. In return, He "is faithful and just and will forgive [me] [my] sins." (1 John 1:9 NIV.) God also has pledged to be with me through all my trials and afflictions, that come from living in a corrupt and imperfect world. God's Word reminds me that I should never fear to be alone again.

I must, however, remember that my adoption came at a very high price—Jesus hung on a cross and bore the shame of my sins, my wrongdoings. It's exciting to know that this is the way God adopts us into His family through Jesus Christ. "This is what he wanted to do, and it gave him great pleasure."

Later as I matured, I discovered that there was indeed a celebration, a time of jubilation, on my adoption day. The Bible tells me in Luke 15:10 (NIV) that "there is rejoicing in the presence of the angels of God over one sinner who repents."

Imagine that—there is a celebration in heaven when we repent and ask Jesus to be our Lord and Savior. Now, imagine the celebration we'll receive when we finally arrive in heaven!

—Juanita Adamson

Quiet Joy

"You make known to me the path of life; you will fill me with joy in your presence, with eternal pleasures at your right hand."
Psalm 16:11 (NIV)

Recently, there's been an influx of thee-year old's into "Little Kidz Church." These precious children no longer consider themselves babies and are the first to tell you so; they are proud to say that they are "big boys and girls." They have finally been potty-trained and given the opportunity to venture out of the safe boundaries of nursery life and enter bravely or, perhaps, not so bravely into the world of "big kids" and "big kid" activities.

One Sunday morning, a three-year-old boy decided he wanted nothing to do with the "big kid" stuff planned for the class. He wasn't interested in friends, modeling clay, puzzles, colors, or anything else offered. What he wanted was simple—he desired nothing more than to be held, a most unusual behavior for this rather rambunctious and adventurous child, independent by nature—but not that day. Perhaps, he needed to feel secure and loved. Who knows what goes on in the mind of a three-year-old!

As the little boy nestled quietly in my lap occasionally laying his head on my shoulder, the Holy Spirit gently reminded me of the times when I need to be held quietly by my Heavenly Father with my head on His shoulder. The times when the child in me wants to sit in complete silence and feel His presence—a short respite from life and its responsibilities and demands—a private time especially selected for me to experience the Lord's love and protection. A rare moment when I don't need a prayer answered, a problem solved, healing, an inspiration, a lesson, or a blessing. I ask for nothing more than to enjoy the solitude, the "quiet"—to be filled "with the joy of [His] presence," and the soft, gentle feeling of love and the refuge of His embrace in our "quiet" moment together.

Have you ever felt the quiet "joy of [His] presence?" It's awesome!

—Juanita Adamson

Don't Steal My Quiet!

"Submit yourselves, then, to God. Resist the devil, and he will flee from you."
James 4:7 (NIV)

One hot July afternoon as my husband and I returned home from shopping, a most unwelcome visitor met us. I was walking toward our front door when I spied the intruder. I froze! An ear-piercing sound, rivaling any operatic star, escaped my throat. My husband rushed to me and asked, "what's wrong?" I pointed and squeaked out, "snake!" In our doorway was a "huge" (my perspective) serpent trying to hide behind a small wooden box. I had frightened it with my blood-curdling scream because it was now totally out of sight. After finding the snake, my husband quickly dispensed with it—a harmless bull snake. It was then that I discovered my "quiet," was gone—the interloper had stolen it.

Later recalling that unsettling afternoon, the Holy Spirit showed me how we should react to sin. When I saw the snake, I stopped and refused to go any closer—I believed I was in immediate danger. My next response was to get away as quickly as possible. That should be our reaction to sin—stop and run in the opposite direction hurriedly because we are in danger! But at times, we behave quite differently.

We know that we should not indulge in sin, yet often we embrace it and, perhaps, even enjoy it for a season. We know that it is wrong and that it will hurt us, and ultimately destroys the "quiet" of our souls—our relationship with the Lord.

The Bible clearly illustrates that our Heavenly Father hates sin and that there are always consequences—penalties to the gossip we repeated, the lies we told, and the indiscretions we committed. The Bible tells us to "Resist the devil, and he will flee from you." The devil is the originator of sin. His sole mission is to destroy us by tempting us to disregard God's Word and do whatever we want. And, just like the snake caused me distress and stole my "quiet" temporarily, sin will result in death if we fail to deal with it by repenting. It will not only steal but destroy the "quiet" of our souls.

—Juanita Adamson

Wet Kiss

"This is what the Sovereign LORD, the Holy One of Israel, says:
"In repentance and rest is your salvation,
in quietness and trust is your strength..."
Isaiah 30:15 (NIV)

One rare rainy winter Arizona morning, I spied a small "painted rock" sitting on a planter near the exit doors of the Sierra Vista Mall. The rock was part of the latest national craze of leaving decorated stones for others to find as bits of encouragement—bringing smiles and humor to the finder's life.

Little did the benefactors know how much I needed encouragement that morning. There is no doubt that silly rock was meant for me. I believe my Heavenly Father orchestrated its placement. Many people walked by in the light drizzle, and no one seemed to notice it. In fact, after spotting the rock, I, too, walked away. Then I felt the Holy Spirit prompt me to go back and pick it up. To my utter surprise, the rock had a pair of lips, garishly painted red, white teeth and the word, KISS, printed above the bizarre lips. When I reached my car with the dripping wet rock in hand, my sagging spirit was lifted. I laughed at this unlikely reminder of God's love for me—it was like a soggy wet kiss from my Heavenly Father.

As I drove home, I began to realize that my disappointments and hurts are only small irritations in comparison to what Jesus endured on the cross for me. He willingly gave his life for my sins, for our sins, without any hesitation or complaint. Yes, I was disappointed and hurt! I felt betrayed, and there was nothing I could do to change the situation. Frustrated and angry were good words to describe my mood. However, with the reminder from heaven, my feelings and perspective were quickly and quietly changed.

When I picked up the rock with the gaudy painted red lips, I was gently reminded that God has everything under control—"repentance and rest is [my] salvation, in quietness and trust is [my] strength." In other words, trust God in everything for He is my (our) strength. After all, He loves us and knows what is best for us. Often, He does His best work unobtrusively.

—Juanita Adamson

Quiet

Every summer my grandchildren from town come and spend a weekend
with us on the cattle ranch. The ranch is on an isolated mountain, several miles
out on a dirt road. One evening, we finished doing the chores—feeding the
horses their hay, putting the chickens in their house, and making sure every
animal had water. As I walked back down the trail, my oldest granddaughter
stopped and said with awe, "Nani, it's so quiet out here I can even hear the
quail chattering as they nest for the night. I can even hear the nighthawk
calling down the road, and the horses munching their hay."

It's true. The chickens were fussing as they made their way to roost, and
the feisty little hummingbirds were sipping at the feeders before they settled in
their favorite tree. But in all those sounds, there was quiet. My granddaughter
discovered that quiet doesn't mean no sound; it means peace in the sounds.

Whether we are listening to the night sounds on the ranch, the sounds of
traffic outside our window in town, the thunder of an evening storm in the
desert or the constant noise of chatter in a restaurant there is quiet if we but
listen.

Just as Jesus needed quiet and asked his disciples to come with Him to
a place of quietness, so do I. Sometimes, the quiet is unexpected as in the
evening at the ranch. And those unexpected times are perfect to hear from
God. We need to stop and listen—stirring honey in our teacup—turning the
pages of a good book—or hearing the wind in the trees.

—Terry Hunt Crowley

Quiet the Mind

"I have so much more to say, but you cannot absorb it right now.
The Spirit of truth will come and guide you in all truth.
He will not speak His own words to you; He will speak what He hears,
revealing to you the things to come and bringing glory to Me.
The Spirit has unlimited access to Me, to all that I possess and know,
just as everything the Father has is Mine. That is the reason
I am confident He will care for My own and reveal the path to you."
John 16:12-15 (The Voice)

Last winter, my husband and I were shopping in a local store where I spotted two large coffee mugs. One had the following saying, "Quiet the mind and the soul will speak." Without hesitation, I bought them—the word "quiet" was boldly imprinted on one. I stated loudly, "that's confirmation, 'quiet' is my word!" Now, what was I going to do with it—what was God going to teach me? Those were the questions, that began ruminating in my mind.

Approximately a year later, while we were drinking tea, lemon, and honey as a relief for bronchitis, I realized the statement on the cup was all wrong! It should say, "Quiet the mind, and God will speak to the soul." It was a late night, "ah ha moment" for me! It was as if God was saying you can't hear me because you are trying to figure and work everything out your way. Because you're busy listening to what you think or what the world is saying, you can't hear what I'm saying. Your mind is cluttered with thoughts not from me, that you cannot hear me over all that racket. It's not until you "quiet" your mind and meditate on my Word, on me, that the Holy Spirit will reveal "to you the things to come" and bring glory to me. Then, in the "quiet" of your soul, I can "reveal the path to you." Suddenly, I was thankful that God had chosen the word, "quiet" for me.

Was it a coincidence that I found those cups? No, I don't think so—it was part of God's plan for me. Do I understand why the word "quiet" was given to me? Yes, I believe it's becoming more evident. It has been an incredible journey as God has patiently taught me the value of "quiet" in my life!

—Juanita Adamson

Quiet Nature

*"The LORD, your God is with you, the Mighty Warrior who saves.
He will take great delight in you; in his love he will no longer rebuke
you but will rejoice over you with singing."*
Zephaniah 3:17 (NIV)

I hated it—my face was turning bright red! Why couldn't I stop it? Most of my life, I have struggled with a lack of self-confidence. As a young teen, I was plagued with extreme shyness and blushing—sometimes for no reason at all. What made matters worse was when someone noticed my crimson face and brought attention to it. Feeling powerless to control what was happening, tears would suddenly roll down my cheeks. People would attempt to explain my response by remarking that it was just part of my "quiet" shy nature. That explanation certainly did not justify the pain that the blushing and shyness caused—not to a 13-year old girl.

As I matured, I realized that crying made the situation worse. But I didn't know how to stop the tears either. Sometime in early adulthood, I inexplicably stopped blushing, but self-confidence was still a raging battle, I fought daily. On the advice of a well-meaning college professor, I took a public speaking class. I was a horrible wreck! My heart felt like it would leap out of my chest each time I gave a presentation. I persevered, completing the class with a decent grade. It would be great to say that the course solved my problem, but it didn't.

As I look back, I realize I didn't understand that God loved me just the way I was—I didn't even know that He cared! I only knew that others weren't fighting the same battle. I didn't recognize God had purposely created in me, a "quiet" and introverted nature because it pleased Him—it fit his plan! I did not know that He takes "great delight in [me]" and "rejoices over [me] with singing."

I admire those who are comfortable speaking to strangers or speak with ease to groups of people. I am content with who I am! And, with that contentment, has come the confidence that it's ok for me to be "quiet" and introverted. Why? Because that is how God created some of us for His purposes. "He will take great delight" in us—whether He has made us introverts, extroverts or ambiverts.

—Juanita Adamson

QUIETNESS AND TRUST WILL
BE OUR STRENGTH

Impossible to Keep Quiet

"You have restored my honor. My heart is ready to explode, erupt in
new songs! It's impossible to keep quiet! Eternal One,
my God, my Life-Giver, I will thank You forever."
Psalm 30:12 (The Voice)

One Thursday morning at the local nursing facility, a 100-year old resident requested her favorite hymn, "I'll Fly Away."[2] She explained that the song book just fell open to the hymn as she opened it. There was no need for an explanation—she frequently requests that particular hymn. In fact, the song is lovingly referred to by the nursing home ministry team as "Connie's favorite hymn."

As the singing began, I looked across the room and noticed her sweet little face light up. I imagined it looked like she was looking into the face of Jesus. Tension and weariness were mysteriously gone; her radiant face looked expectant. Her expression was evidence that her heart was "ready to explode" with love for God as she sang praises to Him. Although she has probably sung "I'll Fly Away" hundreds of times in her lifetime, it was as if she was singing it for the very first time—a new song to her Savior, making it impossible for her "to keep quiet!" I suspect that over her many years, the hymn has become more than a mere song to her. Connie has made it a prayer as she awaits the day when she will fly away to her heavenly home, where she will spend eternity thanking and praising God.

Later, as I reflected on that morning, I realized I want that kind of love for Jesus. Each time I worship, each time I think of Him, I want my heart to be ready "to explode," to "erupt in new songs,"—love songs. When I sing, even those songs and choruses, sung countless times, I want to feel like it's my very first time—to sing them as new songs with vibrancy and expectancy. I want the brand of love for my Jesus that is fresh and exciting—a love that makes it "impossible to keep quiet."

—Juanita Adamson

Quiet Is

"...Be still and know that I am God."
Psalm 46:10 (NIV)

Quiet is sitting and watching a sunrise.

Quiet is listening to crickets chirping or an owl hooting on a summer night.

Quiet is watching your child sleeping peacefully.

Quiet is lying awake at night and listening to Dad praying after hearing of his mother's death.

Quiet is sitting on the sofa after a beautiful family Christmas, and everyone is sleeping.

Quiet is watching the snow falling on a moon-lit night.

Quiet is sitting alone in church after the funeral of a loved one.

Quiet is what Christ did while being persecuted and nailed to the cross for my sins.

In all my moments of quiet, I can rejoice in the glories of God, because I know His presence is my comfort.

As a young girl, I can remember bumping around in the kitchen doing this and that, getting involved, and talking a lot. My mom would tell me to sit down and be quiet. When I asked her what she needed to tell me, she would say,

"I did! You were so busy talking; you didn't hear what I was saying."

Is that true of how we are at times? When we pray or talk to God, let us not be so busy talking or crying, that we are not quiet enough to hear what He has to say.

—Cynthia Beckwith

Weaned

"Surely I have calmed and quieted my soul, Like a weaned child
with his mother; Like a weaned child is my soul within me."
Psalm 131:2 (NKJV)

Because God often uses unorthodox times and methods to teach us the unexpected and the profound, I gained a new appreciation of the word, "quiet"—my word for a season. It seemed that the deaths of several family members and friends occurred in a relatively short period of time. Despite my grief and sadness, God provided examples of what it means to "quiet" the soul.

As the memorial service for a friend began, it was as if God whispered in my ear, "pay attention." I listened intently to the dad of the deceased young woman, present her eulogy. I heard him say in an emotion-filled voice, focusing on the goodness of God, "this is not the path of life I would have chosen, but this is the path my Heavenly Father has chosen for me."

A few months later, at another young women's funeral, I listened to another dad deliver his daughter's eulogy and use it to glorify our Heavenly Father. In front of his loved ones and his congregation, he poignantly explained that he had never expected or even imagined having to attend his daughter's funeral, but His Heavenly Father had other plans.

In both instances, I recognized men, who had "calmed and quieted [their] soul[s]" like a "weaned child." It was apparent that both men trusted God in their circumstances even though they were suffering deeply. They had not lost their faith in God because they did not understand what He was doing. It did not mean that they were not experiencing the pain of losing a beloved child or that they weren't shedding tears or grieving profoundly. It meant that their trust and faith in God was greater than the pain of their loss—their souls filled with God's "quiet" presence.

Since then, I have contemplated on what the two dads said and on Psalm 131:2. I have come to understand that to enjoy God's "quiet" in my soul, I must fully trust that whatever happens to me has been filtered through God's hands. He has my best interest in mind when He allows it to occur. I must never forget that He will be with me through the terrible circumstances because He has promised never to leave or forsake me. And, God always keeps His promises.

—Juanita Adamson

Quietly Waiting

He says, "Be still, and know that I am God;"
Psalm 46:11 (NIV)

God wants His children to be still—be quiet—and wait for Him; then He will calm our hearts in the depths of confusion and quiet our thoughts.

He is the Lord God Almighty. He sees us and loves us so much He sent His Son to save us from an eternity of suffering. He rejoices over us with gladness and singing.

How great is our God? We can't even fathom the depths of the loving care He has for us. I know this is true because of the many trials I have endured with the loss of my loved ones. When you don't know how to pray, read His Word, and wait quietly before the Lord, He will bring you through. He will send His Holy Spirit in the midst of the storm and give us peace as we lift our hands and heart to Him and wait.

Be quiet—do not fear. Let His peace flood your soul and heart in the trial. You will come out refined as gold.

—Rosemary Raptis

Study To Be Quiet

"And that ye study to be quiet, and to do your own business,
and to work with your own hands, as we commanded you."
1 Thessalonians 4:11 (KJV)

Did you know the Bible tells us that we must "study to be quiet?" I didn't know, so I was surprised! I immediately thought—oh, a person is just "quiet." It's a characteristic, a trait—you don't have to study! It's not like learning a language or math. It comes naturally. Why would you have to study? What a conundrum—one that I wanted to figure out.

God quickly provided an example of the need to "study to be quiet." I overheard someone complaining about the songs at a recent Sunday service. They were not to their liking. I wanted to correct them—to give them my take on worship—to remind them that worship is not about them and what they like but about God, who is worthy of our honor and praise.

I was poised and ready when the Holy Spirit prompted me to be "quiet" and to pray for them instead. Instantly, I realized it was not my job, but the Holy Spirit's job to convict them, if necessary. At times, we try to take on the role of the Holy Spirit and speak out instead of "zipping our lips." However, being who we are, we often fail to think or listen to His voice and go right on ahead, giving others a piece of our mind, at times with disastrous results.

How many disagreements, hurt feelings, and fractured relationships could we have avoided if we had been "quiet" and listened to the Holy Spirit? "Study to be quiet" means that we must strive—make it our ambition to lead "quiet" lives and not be the source of conflict and strife, especially in things, that, in the final analysis, don't matter or are none of our business.

As we "study to be quiet," we become more in tune with what God is speaking to us, making it possible for us to live more harmoniously with others.

—Juanita Adamson

Smile

"If I say, 'I will forget my complaint, I will change my expression, and smile..."
Job 9:27 (NIV)

What does your face show? Does it radiate with the joy of the Lord? Is there an expression of love, or wonder on it? Or does it show fear, hurt, disappointment, sadness, or even hatred? It's amazing just how much our facial expressions tell others what we're feeling or thinking without uttering a sound. Expression is a "quiet" movement of muscles under the facial skin. Some say that these movements give away an individual's emotional state, a form of nonverbal communication.

The Lord in the book of Genesis 4:6 (NIV), asked Cain, "Why are you angry? Why is your face, downcast?" God didn't have to look at Cain's heart; his face spoke volumes—his disgust with his brother and the Lord's acceptance of his offering. In the title Scripture above, Job, on the other hand, said, "If I say, 'I will forget my complaint, I will change my expression and smile.'" Job, the man who lost everything, was willing to change his attitude, "forget [his] complaint." He knew the secret of a smile, of that "quiet" expression on his face, revealing his relationship with God.

Thanking God and smiling are not only testaments of our gratitude and inner strength, but, good for our physical health. Smiling is said to lower blood pressure, relieve stress, strengthen our immune system, and lessen pain. It has also proven to be contagious. Smile and see what response you receive from others. We may not be able to control how beautiful we are, but we can control our expression—we can choose to smile or to frown. It's up to us to spread the joy of the Lord, even on those days when everything is going wrong, and we don't feel like smiling.

So, let's send out "quiet" messages of joy today—SMILE. Who knows, it might be just what someone needs.

—Juanita Adamson

Addiction

He says, "Be still, and know that I am God…"
Psalm 46:10 (NIV)

Are we addicted to noise? Yes, many of us are! There are those, who upon awaking, turn on the radio or television; they seem to need noise to be able to function. Others sleep with ambient music or sounds. We are constantly bombarded by noise—in our homes, traffic, malls, restaurants, offices, and a myriad of other places. Even in those areas where talking is not permitted, the hum of electronic equipment is ever present. It seems that there is no respite, no quiet, from the never-ending din of today's world.

I recall being the last one in my office and feeling a sense of reprieve from the daily office clamor. All the electronic equipment was turned off—phones stopped ringing; no employees were there—the only thing that could be heard was the tick of the clock. Instantly, I felt my whole being relax. And, for a few minutes, I enjoyed the sound of "quiet."

Psalm 46:10 tells us to "be still," to be quiet. When noise constantly assaults us, we find it difficult, if not impossible, to hear God's voice? Not only does noise affect our spiritual health; it also affects our physical health and wellbeing. Noise is known to cause hypertension, higher stress levels, hearing loss, sleep disturbances, and other health problems. Noise often makes us irritable and affects our ability to make good decisions.

What is the solution? We can take control and wean ourselves from noise— turn off the radio, television, cell phone, or other distractions. Carefully carve time out of our schedules to be alone with the Lord and then quietly bask in His presence. No talking or music needed. Just you and the Lord—simply "be still."

—Juanita Adamson

Music

It was late October of 2017 when I started asking, "Are you sure, Lord?" The word **Music** was etched in my mind and soon became a burning ember from deep within. But I didn't understand what I was supposed to do—write a song or another poem, maybe? Surely not to sing a special in Church! Within a few months, the Lord put an amazing group of women in my path, The Women Of Grace Writers. In a short time, we formed a close sisterhood, a special bond that could only be of God's design. However, it still wasn't clear what I was to do about my word **Music**, God so strongly impressed upon me. Soon I learned each lady was to write 14 devotions for an up-coming devotional. The Holy Spirit had given each one a special word on which to write. I questioned again, louder this time, "Are you sure it's me you want? You know Lord, I can't even *read* music!"

As I continued this inspired writing endeavor, I FINALLY stopped questioning and started praying! I wanted to study God's Word more in depth to learn what He has to share regarding music. Each day through prayer and Bible study, my eyes became wide open, and a lot was revealed to me.

Within these few pages, you are invited to embrace life
as an inspiring symphony and God as the Divine Conductor.

Freedom

*"...If you abide in My word, you are My disciples indeed.
And you shall know the truth, and the truth shall make you free."*
John 8:31-32 (NKJV)

Last year Ralph and I celebrated the 4th of July by attending "A Parade of American Music" at my friend Billie Hayes' Church. After the Pledge of Allegiance, we sang great patriotic songs—The Star-Spangled Banner, America The Beautiful, God of Our Fathers, and The Battle Hymn of the Republic. Everyone was overjoyed by the melodic cello, trumpets, organ, and piano. I sat with an immense fulfillment as they played a Service Music Medley from each of the military branches. All veterans were asked to stand when their service anthem was played. This undeniably captivated my heart as I witnessed brave US Army, Navy, Air Force and Marine veterans standing proud. There were smiles and admiration on every attendee's face. The applause of honor resounded throughout the sanctuary—what a symbol of our United States patriotism. At that moment, with head held high, I seemed to sit up a little straighter in my seat. I was proud to be an American!

As we celebrated those courageous service men and women, I contemplated the many sacrifices made for our country's liberties. In America, we have the freedom to make the choices and decisions we believe will make all our dreams come true. But God tells us in Scripture of a more profound freedom—the ultimate freedom made available through His Son Jesus Christ. This freedom is an abundant gift, for all people; however, we must each *choose* to accept it!

When I think of the beautiful music and words in the patriotic songs, they can never compare with the moving words Jesus spoke in John 8:36 (NKJV), *"Therefore if the Son makes you free, you shall be free indeed."*

WOW... Praise God! I'm glad to be a Christian—Free to live for HIM!

—Paula J. Domianus

The B - I - B - L - E

*"The whole Bible was given to us by inspiration from God and is useful
to teach us what is true and to make us realize what is wrong in our lives;
it straightens us out and helps us to do what is right.
It is God's way of making us well prepared at every point,
fully equipped to do good to everyone."*
2 Timothy 3:16-17 (TLB)

Someone very special told me long ago that everything about life and living is found in God's Word—The Bible. One of the first songs I learned in Sunday School was called "**THE B-I-B-L-E.**"[3]

The first and second verse goes like this:

> **"The B-I-B-L-E, yes that's the book for me. I stand
> alone on the word of God, the B-I-B-L-E."
> "The B-I-B-L-E, I'll take along with me. I'll read
> and pray and then obey the B-I-B-L-E."**

The Bible reveals God's truth to us and is proof He is, beyond doubt, the Alpha and the Omega, the beginning and the end, the first and the last and everything in between. We should dive deep into His Word—read, pray, study, and learn from it every day!

The following words on the first pages of my pocket-size New Testament are:

"The Bible contains the mind of God, the state of man, the way of salvation, the doom of sinners, and the happiness of believers. Its doctrines are holy, its precepts are binding, its histories are true, and its decisions are immutable. Read it to be wise, believe it to be safe, and practice it to be holy. It contains light to direct you, food to support you, and comfort to cheer you.

It is the traveler's map, the pilgrim's staff, the pilot's compass, the soldier's sword, and the Christian's charter. Here Paradise is restored, Heaven opened…"[4]

Third verse;

**"By F-A-I-T-H, I'm S-A-V-E-D,
I'll stand alone on the word of God, The B-I-B-L-E."**

Through these simple childhood musical lyrics, I
learned the importance of God's Holy Word!

—Paula J. Domianus

In The Garden

"The birds of the sky nest by the waters; they sing among the branches."
Psalm 104:12 (NIV)

The garden beckons you to come, rest and commune with our Lord.

There is an etched inscription carved deep on the burnished Arizona flagstone at the garden's entry, that reads;

"As you enter through the arbor may you experience God's presence, love, mercy and forgiveness. May the peace of this place surround you."

The small prayer garden is nestled in the corner under the shade of the mesquite tree—in the distance is the sound of a woodpecker hard at work searching for his breakfast with the rat-a-tat-tat on the bark of an old tree stump. As the summer breeze gently sweeps through the rustling leaves, you can hear the quail singing a melody along with their babies chirping in their cozy nests. God's presence and majesty surround this tranquil place and elicits all of nature's senses. The breathtaking fragrance of honeysuckle, lavender, and sweet rosemary brings the garden to life. The beauty of the soft pink roses, yellow poppies, and Morning Glories make a stunning presentation. There is a peaceful calming effect as the water flows from the fountain and puddles in the pond. The early morning dew is fresh and glistens off the English Ivy rambling atop the south wall. The light and dark shadows dance across the espaliered Pyracantha, which is an enchanting masterpiece all its own.

God is sovereign over all heaven and earth, and the very existence of nature holds us in awe, not only in sight but sound. The peaceful garden is flourishing with His wonderment beyond expression. I hope that you will experience God's provision and all its glory with a tender heart—spend some quiet time in your garden. Let your spirit soar with amazement and take pleasure in the songbirds—they are God's delightful choir. And if you listen hard enough, you can hear their exceptional song. It's a morning message of love—they are singing and performing a heavenly gala just for you!

—Paula J. Domianus

Let's Celebrate

"And she will bring forth a Son, and you shall call His name Jesus,
for He will save His people from their sins."
Matthew 1:21 (NKJV)

It was an unforgettable Christmas in 1994, full of wonderful memories. Excitement abounded as I prepared for my sister and her three young children's visit. The large nativity scene was proudly displayed on the front balcony, white lights lined the driveway, and red poinsettias adorned the courtyard. All the presents were under the tree, and the aroma of pine scented candles filled the air. Everything was in order, the shopping, decorating, baking, and meal planning complete.

As a family tradition every year, I made a birthday cake for Dad since he was born on December 25th and the cake was our dessert on Christmas Day. It so happened, our little dog Tuffy was also born on Christmas. We commented on "what great company" both were in, as that was when baby Jesus was born.

Our youngest niece, Raven, had just turned four and asked her mom to please leave a note telling Santa she'd be at Aunt Paula's house this year. Little kids bring such great joy, especially during Christmas time! After dinner when we brought out the cake, blazing with all the candles, Raven jumped up with enthusiasm, clapped her hands and squealed, "Oh boy we get to sing Happy Birthday to Jesus!" That moment my heart leaped as I was reminded by a small child how to truly celebrate CHRIST in Christmas.

Dad and Tuffy are no longer with us. All the nieces and nephews are grown and live elsewhere. So, these days, we don't always have a cake on Christmas, but if we do, it says in great big capital letters HAPPY BIRTHDAY JESUS! Now we celebrate Him, thank Him and sing His praises every day all year long, not just on December 25th.

He is no longer a baby in the manger—He is our Lord and Savior—Jesus Christ, who died for us and has given us the greatest gift of all, our salvation!

Let's rejoice and make music from our hearts to the Lord!

—Paula J. Domianus

Power

"Be exalted, O Lord, in Your own strength! We
will sing and praise Your power."
Psalm 21:13 (NKJV)

Are music and singing important to God? Yes, it must be *very important*, as both are accentuated throughout the Old and New Testaments. Music is one of God's creations, and everything He created pleases Him. Music is powerful and has the capability of communicating the gospel to all people. God's music surpasses language, age, space, and moments in time. Through song, our grateful hearts celebrate, worship, praise, glorify, and thank our Lord. We read in Psalm 96:1-3 (NIV), *"Sing to the Lord a new song; sing to the Lord, all the earth. Sing to the Lord, praise his name; proclaim his salvation day after day. Declare his glory among the nations, his marvelous deed among all peoples."*

Music plays an essential part in all our lives and is a beautiful harmonic journey God has planned for us. As a little girl, I was afraid of water, so Momma sang to keep me calm while she washed my hair. In the middle of the night, if a bad dream awakened me, she would hold me close and rock me to sleep with a sweet lullaby. Even now, as an adult, I marvel how God's music continues to bring peace and comfort to me in times of despair. His music has a calming effect; it warms our hearts, soothes our soul, and quiets our spirit. I love the scripture in Zephaniah 3:17 (NKJV), which says, *"The Lord your God in your midst, The Mighty One, will save; He will rejoice over you with gladness, He will quiet you with His love, He will rejoice over you with singing."*

We realize not everyone is designed to be a musician, a famous vocalist, or perform at Carnegie Hall. However, we are all created in God's image to enjoy and be filled with delight through pleasant melodies. By His power and authority, God speaks to us in many ways, and music is one of those avenues.

Can you recall a special time when God's music
lifted you higher than you could imagine?

—Paula J. Domianus

A Father's Love

"Let the little children come to me, and do not hinder them, for the kingdom of heaven belongs to such as these."
Matthew 19:14 (NIV)

William David MacDonald was one of God's "Special Needs Children", who had an inspiring contagious laugh and his own extraordinary way of communicating. He was the first-born child to his God-fearing parents, who loved and cared deeply for all four of their sons. At an early age, it became evident Billy needed a special environment, one that could help him learn to cope. After much prayer and family discussions, Forrest and Peg reluctantly placed young Billy, in a New York State home.

They eventually moved to Arizona and could only communicate by telephone. It seemed, Billy grew in stature, but his gentle spirit remained childlike. This sweet innocent "Special Child of God" soon lost his ability to respond. As time passed, he no longer recognized his father's voice on the phone. The staff informed Forrest that Billy was not doing well and might not live through the night. What was a father to do? He did the only thing he could think of—he sang! The orderly said it was a miracle! The minute Billy heard his father singing on the loudspeaker, he was full of joy and tranquility.

For months there had been no facial expressions, but suddenly he became alert as he recognized his favorite song with Forrest's rich baritone singing voice sounding loud and clear,

"Oh, where have you been, Billy Boy, Billy Boy, where have you been charming Billy?"[5]

A big smile came upon Billy's face and he was consoled. He then turned on his side and shortly after that took his last earthly breath. He found perfect peace, the kind of peace that can only come from the love of our Father in Heaven. This precious boy had a lifetime of adversity but was now able to rest as he journeyed to his glorious eternal home.

How comforting, the last sound Billy heard in this world was his earthly father's voice, and the next would be his Heavenly Father's voice.

—Paula J. Domianus

My Hero

"...Our Father which art in heaven, Hallowed be thy name. Thy kingdom come. Thy will be done in earth, as it is in heaven. Give us this day our daily bread. And forgive us our debts, as we forgive our debtors. And lead us not into temptation, but deliver us from evil: For thine is the kingdom, and the power, and the glory, for ever. Amen."
Matthew 6:9-13 (KJV)

Aunt Jo and Uncle Ed's house was my second home all during childhood. You could tell Uncle Ed put God first in his life, which meant there was always plenty of love to go around. He inspired me, and with great admiration, I would say, "When I grow up, I want to be exactly like my Uncle Ed." He was just as comfortable cooking in the kitchen as he was building projects in his workshop. He walked softly and carried a coffee pot in one hand and an electric drill in the other. He's "My Hero!" He was so clever; he could even *dance* on roller skates (backward no less). My cousin, Sheri, and I had the best-dressed dolls in Bisbee, Arizona, because Uncle Ed designed all their clothes. He walked softly and carried a pair of roller skates in one hand and a needle & thread in the other. He's "My Hero!"

Uncle Ed instilled within me very sound advice. At an early age, I learned prayer was essential. His God-given talents were used to serve the Lord, and for many years he was the revered choir director in our church. This man of God left his footprint ever so gently upon my heart. He walked softly and carried his Bible in one hand and his songbook in the other. He's "My Hero!"

When Ralph and I got married, "My Hero" lovingly sang the Lord's Prayer at our wedding. It was the most wondrous thing I had ever heard. Uncle Ed's voice was most certainly a gift from above. There is a glorious awareness when God's Holy Word, the Bible, is put to melody. The Lord's Prayer is an inspiring Scripture that comes alive through the grandeur of the music. Worshiping by singing the Scriptures is as marvelous a blessing as praying the Scriptures.

—Paula J. Domianus

MUSIC IS A HEAVENLY TREASURE
GOD HAS BESTOWED UPON US.

Heavenly Mission

"singing psalms and hymns and spiritual songs among yourselves,
and making music to the Lord in your hearts."
Ephesians 5:19 (NLT)

One of the most heartfelt and rewarding spiritual experiences of my life was serving on an overseas mission trip. Training Christians for Ministry International has a foreign facility at Haus Edelweiss, located on a beautiful hillside close to Vienna, Austria. At the first session, we had students from twelve countries speaking many different languages.

During our last worship service, something wonderful occurred. As we all gathered together, I witnessed a little slice of heaven right here on earth. There we all were each from a different region, under one roof, worshiping one God, praising His name and singing "Amazing Grace."[6] As we stood and sang those beautiful words in unison, I could distinguish and understand each foreign language. Instantly, I imagined that's precisely how heaven will be. It was a feeling of sheer love and acceptance as we became one body of believing brothers and sisters in Christ. Glory be to God!

It was on that trip I discovered how much God loves music. He is passionate about it! Music and song are not used only to praise Him, but it is a wonderful way to communicate and teach others His Love. I am reminded of a quote from Martin Luther, the theologian: *"Next to the Word of God, the noble art of music is the greatest treasure in the world."[7]* It gives us encouragement and comfort.

Did you know Jesus even sang? That night in the Upper Room after the Last Supper, He and His disciples sang a hymn before going to the Mount of Olives (Matthew 26:30 and Mark 14:26 NLT). Knowing what suffering lay ahead, Jesus still sang! I wonder by singing, did it make Him feel closer to His Father? And hopefully, it gave Him greater strength to endure the beating and crucifixion that was to come.

Each time we praise God with our song and music, something divine happens—we find ourselves in His glorious presence!

—Paula J. Domianus

Sing Praises to His Greatness

"Great is the Lord, and highly to be praised, And His greatness is
[so vast and profound as to be] unsearchable [incomprehensible to man]."
Psalm 145:3 (AMP)

There are those who say they cannot believe in God because they cannot see Him with their natural eyes. But God and His Greatness have always been obvious to me through His creation.

Blessed to have been born into a Christian home and having come to know Jesus at a very early age, I recall one of my experiences as a young child of about the age of nine. During those years, we would go to visit my grandparents in Alabama. They had a few acres of land and raised a cow and chickens, etc. They had a small graveyard up the hill from their house where my uncle and one of my younger brothers are buried. A big part of my dad's family would gather at my grandparent's home on Memorial Day to decorate the graves.

The small house was full of the hustle and bustle of relatives and friends. I often felt the need for some alone time—so I would walk up the small hill to the opposite side of the graveyard. I would lay on my back in the soft grass beneath the big trees to watch the sun twinkling through the wafting leaves—and the breeze cooled me in the shade—I was enjoying the beauty of God's natural blessings. I moved out into the sun closer to the edge of the cliff and knelt in the grass, watching the fluffy white clouds slowly drifting through the expanse of the soft blue sky. My heart swelled with the love of a God, who could create such a beautiful world for us—for me. In whispers of gratitude, I began to sing that beautiful hymn, "How Great Thou Art,"[8] and my tears flowed. What a pivotal experience for me!

Yes, some may find it difficult to believe in a so-called "invisible God" but for me, just merely gazing at the vastness, the beauty, and the variety of His creativity puts me in awe of Him. How can I not believe in Him? How can I not love Him?

For me, He is just as real as all His creations! His love that fills and overflows from my heart is totally real! For me, He cannot be denied, and I will sing His praises with Him throughout eternity!

—Rev. Rebecca J. Fiedler

A Matter Of Minutes

"Solomon composed 3,000 proverbs, and his songs numbered 1,005."
1 Kings 4:32 (HCSB)

We read in 1 Kings 3:12,13 (HCSB) how the Lord blessed Solomon with wisdom, riches, honor, and gave him an understanding heart. The Song of Solomon is the best of Solomon's musical works, which was written under divine inspiration and is full of poetic songs that honor the Lord. Also known as Song of Songs—it provides spiritual music for a beautiful harmonious marriage.

Today, writers sometime receive what is known as a "given verse." Poets often experience this as well as many songwriters. Some may refer to it as "a God thing," and it most definitely is from God. It's as though a still small voice from within has a perfect message for only you to hear. As these words are forming, there is a burning desire to write them down. You have absolutely no time to think—you start writing as fast as you can because the phrases are coming at rapid speed. I have experienced this phenomenon only twice in my lifetime—a poem called "Thy Will Be Done," published in 1997[9] and another poem titled "Quest." I believe these are special sonnets, gifts of love bestowed upon us from God's favor, that we should express for His honor and His glory.

One night many years ago, Stuart Hamblen was awakened at midnight. Words were spinning around in his head, so he got up, turned on the light, grabbed his pen and paper, and started writing. Within a few minutes, he wrote the beautiful song "It Is No Secret" (What God Can Do).[10] He not only wrote the lyrics in a matter of minutes but all the musical notes as well. As Stuart shared his story, one evening at a church meeting, a little lady stood up and said, "Sonny, you didn't really write that song at all. You only got to hold the pen!"[11] Can you imagine? What an honor!

God can use you beyond belief;
are you listening, is that still small voice speaking to you?

—Paula J. Domianus

Quest

—⚬⟡⚬—

"It is the Lord who goes before you. He will be
with you; he will not leave you or
forsake you. Do not fear or be dismayed."
Deuteronomy 31:8 (ESV)

"God still loves me" was something I kept repeating over and over trying to reassure myself, but why did I feel so unworthy and alone? I was searching for answers about life and continuously looking for a sign from above. While driving to work on that stretch of road from Bisbee to Sierra Vista, Arizona, I watched and waited for a sign. Every day for weeks, I yearned for something, any little thing to remind me God was still in His heaven. Why couldn't He show me a burning bush? I would have settled for a small tumbleweed ablaze on Highway 90.

Then one day it happened! I believe God gave me His sign! The most brilliant rainbow arched over the Mule Mountains. Sure, I had witnessed plenty of rainbows before, but this time, it was different, very different! It was as though the Holy Spirit was whispering poetic words in a rhythmic tone coming from the magnificent colors of the rainbow. I stopped on the side of the road, and as I felt His very presence, in haste, I penned these words:

"Have you never sought a rainbow, reached out to touch the wind
quivered and been afraid in constant search of a friend

Have you never looked at a baby and a teardrop come to the eye
watched the sunset with rolling clouds that pass us by

Have you never felt any sorrow for things that were said
wondered about life and living or ways it's led

Have you never shared your secrets and found a warm content
laughed or been happy over the years you've spent

Have you never dreamed of the universe, if only to touch a falling star
thanked God simply for loving you just as you are"[12]

As tears began to flow, I wondered how I could have ever doubted God's love for me. Regardless of our circumstances, He will never leave us or forsake us! Suddenly, I found myself humming that inspirational praise song *"His Love Endures Forever."*[13]

—Paula J. Domianus

The Little Chatterbox

"Enter into His gates with thanksgiving, And into His courts with praise. Be thankful to Him, and bless His name."
Psalm 100:4 (NKJV)

An adorable boy about seven-years-old was sitting directly behind us in church on Sunday. Ryan was visiting his grandmother, Sandy, who was so proud to have her young grandson sitting beside her. Before the church service started, Ryan sat very quietly with a hymnal in hand and smiled as people walked by. With joy, the pastor began, "It's great to be in God's house this morning!" A little voice said, "It's great to be in God's house this morning!" The Pastor bowed his head and continued, "Let's pray together..." Again, it came, "Let's pray together…" And so, it went on through the entire sermon. The repetition was nonstop during communion, the closing prayer, and even announcements. Every word spoken aloud, was repeated by the little boy in the seat behind us.

After the service, Sandy approached us and whispered, "I hope Ryan didn't disturb you, but we encourage him to try and talk as much as possible." I looked a little puzzled and thought, *why would someone do that?*

With a smile and excitement, she said, "His little voice is such beautiful sweet music to my ears! We are so blessed!" She continued to explain that from infancy and until age five, her grandson could only communicate through sign language. Ryan was born with childhood Apraxia—a condition at birth where a child is unable to form words by linking syllables together, and articulation is a problem.

Sandy also shared that he was beginning to read and figure out math problems as a result of attendance in a special school. That day as I left the church, I was so inspired, I sang the "Hallelujah Chorus" all the way home!

What better words than God's Words can a little boy speak. Most certainly, Ryan's sweet little voice is **beautiful music** to God's ears!

—Paula J. Domianus

In Her Room

"And we know that all things work together for
good to those who love God, to those
who are called according to His purpose."
Romans 8:28 (NKJV)

My mother, Charity, was extremely bold in her Christian walk, and salvation was of the utmost importance. For years she sang in the church choir and used her lovely soprano voice to praise God. She spent much of her life witnessing for the Lord, but now she remained quiet and still—powerless to utter a sound. As she lay silently in the nursing home, there was the most indescribable presence in her room.

In the early morning, I would snuggle in beside her on the narrow bed and whisper, "I love you, Momma." I was positive she heard my soft voice and the inspiring music playing in the background. The lyrics were from a song she had written through God's direction some 20 years prior. She had searched unsuccessfully for someone to write the precise music to complement her lyrics. Ultimately, I shared this dilemma with a girlfriend, who composed a piano arrangement and recorded Momma's song, on a Demo CD.

Every day as we played that precious CD—it lifted our spirits and strengthened our faith. Word spread quickly throughout the nursing home and to our amazement, more and more people came in her room to hear the song. The nurses, cleaning team, doctors, friends, and family were all blessed. It seemed the heart-warming music enveloped each person with God's abiding love and peace. I gently kissed her and said, "Momma, your song is making a difference for God's Kingdom!" But I wasn't sure she realized how significant it had become. Then suddenly a little teardrop appeared and slowly ran down her cheek. I knew that instant—she fully understood.

God's grace and mercy shone brightly in her room that day!

The title of her song is "I'm Going Home To Be With Jesus." Lyrics by Charity Blake—music and vocals by Carla Townsend. One sweet day two weeks later, Momma left her room and went home to be with Jesus.

—Paula J. Domianus

Follow Me

*"If you declare with your mouth, "Jesus is Lord," and believe in your heart
that God raised him from the dead, you will be saved.
For it is with your heart that you believe and are
justified, and it is with your mouth
that you profess your faith and are saved."*
Romans 10:9,10 (NIV)

I must have played that old record a hundred times but not until one night in my lonely apartment did I understand it's meaning—I finally got it! The song was "Follow Me"[14] and as I listened not only with my ears but with my heart the words resonated from the depth of my soul. The spectacular image of that night is something I will carry with me forever. It was so miraculous, I do not know the earthly words to honorably describe it, only that my life has never been the same.

With God's loving grace, He sent His Son that night, and in some manner, Jesus corresponded throughout and around my entire being. The extraordinary experience of gladness and inner joy, simultaneously combined with tears of grief, brought me to my knees. I was mindful of why I was sad and weeping because I felt such deep remorse for the sin in my life. Then the delight, along with pure joy, overtook my body with the awareness of God's divine love and forgiveness. As I bowed my head and looked down, it seemed like my hardened heart had shattered into thousands of tiny pieces. Warm radiant light filled the room. I believed I witnessed Jesus' nail-pierced hands glowing in front of me, and the nail holes appeared to be darkened areas close toward His wrists. It was as if those precious hands tenderly gathered each piece of my broken heart and gave me a new loving heart, one that reflects God's, own heart. There were no words spoken. The only communication was by light, beautiful, exquisite light! While kneeling in the midst of my brokenness, I repented of my sin. Soon after that, during a worship service, I humbly accepted the greatness of eternal salvation and was baptized into Christ.

Beloved, my prayer is you will open your heart, receive and walk
in the blessed assurance of God's saving grace
and ***follow Him*** all the days of your life.

—Paula J. Domianus

Watch

As I concentrated on the word WATCH I questioned whether God was saying to me that I needed to watch how I was living my life (a scary thought), to watch for the prophetic signs of the times, to be more attentive to the needs of others, or just to "wake up and smell the coffee."

Whatever HIS specific reason, this has been a glorious spiritual journey of research, prayer, soul-searching, and intimate fellowship with my Heavenly Father.

I pray that the inspirational writings in this section will encourage you, as the reader, to watch for a message—a teachable moment from God—every day and every moment of your life.

Watch

"Take ye heed, watch [be alert] *and pray; for ye know not when the time is.
For the Son of man is as a man taking a journey, who left his house, and
gave authority to his servants, and to every man his work, and commanded
the porter to watch… Lest coming suddenly, he find you sleeping…"*
Mark 13:33-36 (KJV)

When our ministry team goes to the local care center to provide a praise and worship service for the residents—we often need to adjust the volume of the microphones. We tap on the mic several times until the right volume has been achieved for everyone to hear—while continually repeating, "can you hear me now—can you hear me now?" The residents' responses are seen in their grimace when the sound is too low—but then their gigantic smiles when "we are coming through loud and clear." That is sort of what has happened in my attempt to write this devotion. God had inspired me to use this scripture, but for some reason His ultimate goal for my concentration on this particular text had not "come through loud and clear for me."

However, as I began to take inventory, I found that in recent years my life has been one giant Post-It Note. It includes daily tasks to be accomplished, but the one that is noticeably missing is a note that should say "get the prayer closet finished (*in red letters no less*)." So, you may ask what does that have to do with the scripture verses shown above? *I'm glad you asked!*

Some time ago, I had the unction to turn my shed in the back yard into a prayer closet—a place to pray, study and write. Accordingly, I had a contractor put in a window and repair the roof to seal and prevent future leaks, but I had not ventured any further to complete the project. So, as with the scenario describing the need to adjust the microphone at the care center, I have determined that I need to adjust my spiritual hearing. That is, that I need to put many "other things" aside and become a better listener (and doer)— "lest coming suddenly He finds *me* sleeping" (or procrastinating – *in my words*).

Therefore, in the midst of our busyness—if or when
we sense our Heavenly Father asking
"Can you hear me now?"—our answer should immediately be

"Speak, LORD; for thy servant heareth" (1 Samuel 3:9 KJV).

—Phyllis Andrews

Final Approach Into Tucson

"...now, it is high time to awake out of sleep: for now is
our salvation nearer than when we believed."
Romans 13:11 (KJV)

There is generally a measure of turbulence as an airplane "slips the bonds of earth" and travels up through the clouds and hopefully, into smoother air.

If you are like me, you lean your head back against the seat, close your eyes and relax and pray as that giant creation of metal and fiberglass rocks and creaks as it glides up through the clouds and the various changes in the atmosphere.

Recently, I heard a pastor explain that the attacks of the *evil one* on our spiritual journeys can sometimes suck the very life out of us—I would agree. They can have us rocking and creaking like taking off in a jumbo jet. Those attacks can also mimic the sensation of the times when an airplane hits an air pocket and drops suddenly like an unpredictable dip on a roller coaster. Then when you manage to recover, you take a deep breath and check your *watch* to calculate the amount of time left in your flight. How much longer will you feel anxious as you wait for the next dip to occur? Remarkably, God gives us indescribable peace and even sleep during those hiccups on our various personal journeys, as well as on our life assignments for His Kingdom.

Gratefully, the sweetest words I wait to hear from the Southwest Airlines' pilot are "prepare for our final approach into Tucson." I breathe a sigh of relief and joyfully stretch out the kinks of being tightly confined in my seat from the long flight. I gather my belongings in anticipation of arriving at my final destination. God has kept me by His grace, and I'm almost home!

Similarly, in this life, when we have persevered in the many journeys and divine appointments for the Lord—through sometimes smooth and sometimes turbulent air—we'll also check our *watches* as we joyfully stretch out the kinks of a life well lived. We will slip the bonds of this life and hear those sweet promised words from our Lord— *"Well done, thou good and faithful servant ... enter thou into the joy of thy lord"* (Matthew 25:21 KJV).

In other words—*Welcome Home!*

—Phyllis Andrews

Watch the Pot

"Do not quench [subdue, or be unresponsive to the
working and guidance of] the [Holy] Spirit."
1 Thessalonians 5:19 (AMP)

A guest on a recent episode of "The 700 Club" television program explained the reason for the title of his newly released inspirational book. The title—"Take The Lid Off"[15]—was a reference to his grandmother's instructions when her pot was boiling over on the stove. The lid restricted the release of steam and heat that had built up in the bubbling stew.

In Jeremiah 20:9 (AMP), the prophet explains this scenario well when he says, *"If I say, 'I will not remember Him or speak His name anymore,' then my heart becomes a burning fire shut up in my bones. And I am weary of enduring and holding it in; I cannot endure it [nor contain it any longer]."*

Similarly, my friend explained the steps for the successful making of one of her recipes called "Posole." She explains that the caution in finishing this soup is that you need to keep the lid off until it has cooled, or the contents will spoil.

As Christians, we are sometimes filled with a special anointing of His Spirit—almost like that pot of boiling stew or soup. He fills us with a holy boldness to openly praise Him or to speak encouraging or thought-provoking words to those within our area of influence. However, we can suddenly entertain a spirit of fear that causes us to "keep the lid on," rather than to obey the Spirit and possibly witness to someone about the saving grace of Jesus Christ.

The Bible says that it is both sinful and dangerous for believers to grieve the Holy Spirit of God (See Ephesians 4:30 KJV). Accordingly, as the Spirit bubbles up and overflows in our lives, He will provide both light and warmth around *us* to draw others to Himself. Therefore, "don't quench the Spirit," but allow Him to work in the lives of others through you!

—Phyllis Andrews

In the Fulness Of Time

*"I will stand upon my watch, and set me upon the tower, and
will watch to see what he will say unto me, ... the vision is yet
for an appointed time, but at the end it shall speak, and not lie:
though it tarry, wait for it; because it will surely come, ..."*
Habakkuk 2:1, 3 (KJV)

Doctor Bobby Schuller, a prominent pastor in California, makes this profound statement that really makes me pause to discern if it is disrespectful to God. He says that "God's timing can be so annoying." I have resolved that this is such a true statement, especially for those of us who trust God and faithfully watch for His answers to our prayers. Sometimes it's almost as intense as "watching paint dry."

The Bible is full of such situations. For example, Abraham and Sarah became frustrated as they waited years before they received their promised son, Isaac. Abraham also prepared to sacrifice this long-awaited son to God (See Hebrews 11:17 KJV) but "in the fulness of time," God provided an animal sacrifice.

The nation of Israel waited thousands of years for the Messiah to be revealed—however, "when the fulness of the time was come God sent forth his Son..." [the promised Messiah into the world] (See Galatians 4:4 KJV). And presently, we are still waiting for the return of that crucified and risen Perfect Redeemer, the Lord Jesus Christ, to come and take us to be with Him forever.

In addition, each year on New Year's Eve, I observe with others (on what is referred to as Watch Night) how the slaves in America watched and waited in 1863 to hear of the signing of the Emancipation Proclamation. They were eager to see some relief from their years of burden.

More recently, the entire world waited and watched and prayed to hear the words "Everyone is safe" with regard to the rescue mission to bring 12 boys and their soccer coach from their treacherous 18-day position in a flooded cave in Thailand.

Yes, God's timing can seem to be annoying when we are
eagerly waiting for a response to our prayers. But surely
the answer will come "and not tarry." I'm a witness!

—Phyllis Andrews

What Is Man?

*"When I consider thy heavens, the work of thy fingers, the moon
and the stars, which thou hast ordained; What is man, that thou
art mindful of him? ... For thou hast made him a little lower than
the angels, and hast crowned him with glory and honour.
O LORD our Lord, how excellent is thy name in all the earth!"*
Psalm 8:3-5, 9 (KJV)

I looked forward to—and enjoyed—a much-needed vacation recently. I left home with my "bucket list" of things to accomplish but told my friend (and traveling companion) that we should just be led by the Holy Spirit in everything we did. We would not rush through this "*God* trip," as we called it. It was so named because we planned to visit the new Museum of the Bible in Washington, DC, the new Noah's Ark Encounter, and the Creation Museum in Kentucky. Also, on this list was to worship at the historic church I had attended in the summer visits to my grandparents' home as a child. This was sandwiched in-between seeing all of my family including two great-grandchildren I had never met. One final thing that *God* added to my list was to try to find out what happened to a little girl we had thought about adopting over 45 years ago.

Our great and mighty God allowed us to put check marks after each stop on my list, except for time to find this "little girl." Accordingly, we assumed that this would be a quest for another trip. However, as we got on the hotel shuttle to the airport for our flight home, we engaged in small talk with the shuttle driver. "Ironically," she knew the family who had raised this little foster child, and she promised to contact them for me on Facebook.

Hmmm, strange hotel, strange driver, strange town, at 3:30 in the morning!

What a conclusion for our supernatural God trip! I was so visibly shaken by this glorious blessing that I whispered this prayer as I held back the tears: "Lord what do you need or want me to do for all of Your amazing goodness to me?"

I believe God answered: "I didn't ask you for anything."

How grateful I am to have lived long enough to
automatically watch for God in every situation.

However, it still amazes me how unbelievably good He is to us.

—Phyllis Andrews

Beauty Marks

*"The Spirit of the Lord GOD is upon Me, Because the LORD has anointed
Me To preach good tidings to the poor; He has sent Me to heal the
brokenhearted...To give them beauty for ashes...That they may be called
trees of righteousness, the planting of the LORD, that He may be glorified."*
Isaiah 61:1, 3 (NKJV)

When I visited my son and his family at their new home in Maryland, I noticed a tree in the side yard that appeared to be struggling to live under the burden of insect infestation and choking vines. A recent picture my son sent me shows that tree flourishing with healthy branches and limbs, and lush foliage, in addition to tremendous growth over the past three years. However, the trunk of the tree shows deep black marks where the vines had been. Those vines were literally sucking the life out of the tree until they were cut and pulled away by their roots.

But, watch God work!

As the title scripture indicates, Jesus came as "The Divine Anointed One" to give us beauty for our ashes—those dead and dying things in our lives. Those things too numerous to itemize that were keeping us from growing spiritually—those things that only we may have known about.

Even as we learn to trust God with our daily lives—as we learn to lay aside those things intended by "the enemy" to destroy us— there still may be noticeable scars (sometimes physical, mental or emotional) that remain even after our salvation is secure through Jesus Christ.

As with the scars on that tree in my son's yard, God will turn your scars into marks of beauty that will glorify Him as you walk in the newness of life.

—Phyllis Andrews

Can You Come Help Us?

"And a vision appeared to Paul in the night; There stood a man of Macedonia, and prayed him, saying, Come over into Macedonia, and help us.
Acts 16:9 (KJV)

The Apostle Paul was a busy man, going from place to place preaching the Gospel of Jesus Christ as he heard and felt the call of God to go. Scriptures following the one shown above indicate that Paul actually responded to that vision and did go to Macedonia and even unto many other cities reaching people for Christ. Paul further writes that "a wide door for effective service has opened to me [i.e., in Ephesus] ..., and there are many adversaries" (See 1 Corinthians 16:9 KJV).

Answering God's call can be another scary thing because we rarely know "what lies ahead."

Not too long ago, while I was waiting for service at the butcher counter of a local grocery store, I had an opportunity to listen to another customer to explain her painful physical condition to me. I was instantly overwhelmed with the desire to pray for her right then, but there were people coming and going close to us, so I just promised to pray for her as she rode away on her scooter. Even though I was obedient and prayed for her later as I had promised, the immediate opportunity to be a blessing to her had already passed.

Also, a man recently called our house twice with a similar request as Paul had heard— "Can someone come help me?" He sounded elderly, and I assumed that he had misdialed our number thinking that he was calling the police department. That number is just one digit different than ours. Even more astounding was that only a few days before those calls, I had a dream of that very scenario.

The world is full of people who are calling out, "can you come help us." Maybe not in words, but clearly in their eyes and through their circumstances. Our calls may not be in the form of a vision or dream, but sometimes by a "still small voice" that encourages us to *do it now*. God has already "set before us a wide-open door for service"—we need to watch for His directions, placing our confidence in Him, and boldly walking through the door.

—Phyllis Andrews

WATCH FOR GOD – "LEST
COMING SUDDENLY
HE FINDS YOU SLEEPING"
(SEE MARK 13:36 – KJV)

For Heaven's Sake

*"He shall call upon me, and I will answer him: I will be with him
in trouble; I will deliver him, and honour him."*
Psalm 91:15 (KJV)

The words of a notable hymn often sung by Ethel Waters during Billy Graham crusades, and written by Mrs. C.D. Martin in 1906, has always been a favorite which I have also sung for many years –

"His Eye is on the Sparrow"[16]— *("and I know He watches me").*

In my opinion, no one else who I've heard sing that song has conveyed the sentiment of the words as well as Ethel Waters. Her book with this title and another crusade edition of the book, "I Touched A Sparrow," written by her close friend, Twila Knaack, both reveal the challenges in life experienced by this sweet-, sultry-, yet husky-voiced singer. She loved the Lord and boldly confessed Him before the world, whether in an airport, a hospital or wherever she was. Her author has noted this comment by Miss Waters:

*"When I sing 'Sparrow,'" I know I'm the sparrow
he watched over all these years."*

Reading the story of her life only reinforces my determination to continue seeking God early and to watch and wait for Him to guide my heart. Too often, I believe that God has had to speak to my heart on the run—as I used to begin my days with my own agenda. But I praise God that He has taught me—and hopefully is teaching you—that He watches over us as He does the sparrow.

He listens for our call and promises to answer in every situation. The story of Ethel Waters' life is a wonderful testimony of how God leads and directs us through challenges that we would never ordain for ourselves. Although her beginning was lowly and sometimes tumultuous, she was ultimately lauded by presidents and preachers, entertainers and so-called nobodies. She could confidently and humbly say that the life she lived was indeed *"for heaven's sake."*

Wow. What an awesome testimony to emulate.

—Phyllis Andrews

Guard Your Heart

"Watch over your heart with all diligence, for from it flow the springs of life."
Proverbs 4:23 (AMP)

Commentaries and study notes on this title scripture indicate that the aim of "the teacher" (Solomon) is to expound on the wisdom of obedience and discipline in our lives. Especially that the reader should guard or watch what is allowed into the innermost part of man (the heart) to ensure that no wicked or dark element can enter to cause anyone to stumble or fall short in their faith. The moral conduct of life is determined by the condition of the heart out of which flows "the springs of life."

Well, I was assured that "I was good" concerning this verse as I have consistently resisted watching offensive television shows or reading off-color books, and avoiding offensive conversations, etc. I always try to avoid shopping where there could be wicked or dark elements sold or even purchasing any clothing that contains images or writing that would be offensive for my Christian walk. However, several years ago, I heard a message by a minister on one of the Christian television channels that called my ears to attention! The minister indicated that we should be certain that we don't even have any items of demonic influence in our homes. Again, I was convinced that "I was also good" in that lane until he cautioned about having any other items in our homes with demonic or evil designs on them—*BINGO!*

The Holy Spirit called my attention to the fact that there were dragons, gargoyles, snakes, etc., on some of the Oriental-Art Deco vases and lamps that I had. Prior to hearing that I had no conviction that those beautiful items could permit any evil into our home, but after I trashed each of those objects, there was a noticeable difference in the atmosphere in our home.

*Please note that these items I found in my house were destroyed
and not merely given to one of the local thrift stores to be sold.*

Accordingly, remember to pray first, then go through each room in your house to weed out any place where "the enemy" can find a sweet resting place. It will make a difference.

—Phyllis Andrews

Not on My Watch

*"Exercise foresight and be on the watch to look [after one another],
to see that no one falls back from and fails to secure God's grace..."*
Hebrews 12:15 (AMPC)

"*A*nd the Lord said unto Cain, where is Abel thy brother? And he said I know not: am I my brother's keeper?" This lesson from Genesis 4:9 (KJV), gives us the familiar story of the deadly confrontation between the first brothers.

The Pulpit Commentary calls this "the gospel of selfishness" that is proclaimed and practiced by the world. The masses often think that the mantra of the day should be "every man for himself and God for us all."

However, in the title scripture above, our Lord reminds us that we are called to care for the welfare of each other. We are to tend to the needs of each other, being "*gentle among you, even as a nurse cherisheth her children*" (1 Thessalonians 2:7 KJV).

Many of us have heard of the fury of a mother bear when she suspects that her cub is being harmed. Well, my first—and similar—such heroic act was my forcible retrieval of my son's briefcase from a 6-foot tall bully who had taken it from him on his way home from elementary school. At least he looked that tall to me. I'm confident that the scene could have made for a great newspaper comic strip, especially since I was only 5'3" tall at the time. I only know that God gave me supernatural strength and the determination that this wasn't going to happen on my watch that day!

My sons and I have laughed many times as we recall my unbridled tirade that day. I believe that we as Christians need to "man up" and boldly face those giants in life, who would intend to harm those who are weak.

Yes, we are certainly our brother's keeper—
but please don't do anything stupid.

First, make sure that the heavenly troops are with you.

—Phyllis Andrews

God Has Forgotten Me?

"But he knoweth the way that I take: when he hath
tried me, I shall come forth as gold."
Job 23:10 (KJV)

This past year was an extremely trying year for me. UGH! I mean—NOTHING was going my way financially. I began to brainstorm and think about the talents and gifts that God had given me, and I invested in these resources. I read countless messages on faith—standing on God's Word, praising God in advance for the victory, and rebuking fear, worry, and doubt.

There was a new job opportunity in my community, closer to home and more money! I invested in my voiceover career and spent money on a professional commercial demo reel. Alas, the new job opportunity didn't pan out, and the demo reel only yielded one client. Besides, my wife lost her job, and my 28-year son lost his job, our air conditioning unit suddenly needed replacing, and the summer job that I possessed for the previous four summers was no longer available. *What in the world!*

I was faithful to prayer, faithful to my wife and children, serving God in my local church in many capacities, serving humanity as an educator, and doing whatever it took to "be there" for everyone else. I seriously began to wonder if God had forgotten me—and my struggles.

Then one morning, as I was praying, I noticed a plant that I have in my dining room. It's a small palm tree-like plant that hasn't grown much during the year that I've had it. I wondered why this tree never seemed to grow or barely show any sign of life. It almost looks plastic! However, on this particular day, I noticed a BEAUTIFUL small white bud that had emerged from the top of the plant. It had oil dripping down onto the other leaves, and it produced a sweet fragrance as well.

I believe the Holy Spirit spoke to me through this incident and reminded me that God HAD NOT forgotten me—that everything we need is already deep within us.

So, don't stop watching, praying, and believing!

—Alan Reed

Watch Your Mouth

"Pride goeth before destruction, and an haughty spirit before a fall."
Proverbs 16:18 (KJV)

When we are abundantly blessed by God, whether financially, intellectually, with physical beauty (attractiveness) or possibly with power and influence, we can have the tendency to become prideful in our achievements. An excellent example is the life of the biblical king, Nebuchadnezzar.

God permitted him to rule over Israel when they were in bondage for many years. His rule and influence had spread to all parts of the earth (See Daniel 4:22 KJV). However, like some of us, he became full of pride in himself to a point where his sin led him to believe that he could sin, oppress his underlings, and live without God. He openly boasted of his mighty power that built up Babylon. Because of his arrogance, God punished him for his pride, which God hates (See Proverbs 6:16-17 KJV). For his offense, Nebuchadnezzar was sentenced to a life of insanity, eating grass and becoming like a beast eating the grass of the fields, and subject to the dew of the earth and air for seven seasons.

Gratefully, when Nebuchadnezzar came to himself and looked up to God, who is the Maker, Organizer, and Controller of everything, he was restored to his former self and glory.

This is a wonderful lesson of redemption. But this story is also a just warning to us to remember where life and blessings come from and to acknowledge God's sovereignty in all that we have and do. Proverbs 27:2 (KJV) also gives us guidance in this regard: *"Let another man praise thee, and not thine own mouth; a stranger, and not thine own lips."*

In God's economy, we are all on the same level in His sight—just with different duties for the kingdom. I don't think I would like the taste of grass or want to drink the dew of the earth as Nebuchadnezzar was assigned to do. So my goal is to be a good steward of all that God has entrusted to me, to watch how I treat others, especially with what I say and how I say it—and ultimately to give Him glory for who He has ordained me to be.

—Phyllis Andrews

P.I.P.

"The Lord will perfect that which concerneth me…"
Psalm 138:8 (KJV)

For a big part of my life, I have suffered from a chronic ailment—P.I.P. (**P**erfectionism-**I**nduced **P**rocrastination.) It was only recently that I was able to put a name to this non-contagious, but thoroughly debilitating disease. I felt I couldn't get things done. I was so busy trying to make everything perfect that many things were being left to complete at the last minute.

However, after living the last twenty-or-so years in Southern Arizona I am learning *to let go* of my compulsion to control the furniture dust, to realize that books don't always have to be absolutely in line with each other on the shelves, and that spots on the windows are pretty much okay until after the monsoon rains have abated. This ailment probably stemmed from my desire to do everything worthy of my parents' approval. Then the fervor grew to try to keep everybody happy—then trying to make sure that God was pleased with my attempt at perfection.

The covenant that we read each first Sunday at my church when I was growing up was wonderful—and it became the mantra for my spiritual life—but it also became another list of "things" that I had to get right. My striving for excellence was also a great work ethic, but it has taken years for me to learn how to slow down and rest. I praise God that through the power of His Holy Spirit, He has been such remarkable help in relieving this stress in my life. However, sadly, with this new-found freedom, I think I have sometimes replaced my P.I.P. issues with a severe case of laziness ☺—or maybe I can blame it on retirement and "the aging process."

I have come to believe that this P.I.P. ailment is one of the slimiest viruses that comes straight from Satan! *Just watch*: Immediately when you are focused and ready to attack a Spiritually inspired project, Satan finds a more pressing issue to which to divert your attention.

But watch! Stay Alert! Don't give in!

I've learned that when I ignore Satan, and take the first step forward, that God will give me the mental energy to stay focused and continue in the right direction.

It is so refreshing now to live the very best life I can—to be steadfast in my calling and work for the Kingdom—then leave the perfecting to "the only Perfect One." *Hallelujah!*

—Phyllis Andrews

I See You

"Then she called the name of the LORD who spoke to her, "You are God Who Sees;" for she said, "Have I not even here [in the wilderness] remained alive after seeing Him [who sees me with understanding and compassion]?"
Genesis 16:13 (AMP)

When my sons were in their highchairs at mealtime, we used to play the "Peek-A-Boo; I See You" game. When I covered my face in the game, it gave them the allusion that I had disappeared. Then when I quickly removed my hands, and they saw my face, they would burst out with laughter. Then cereal and juice were going everywhere.

Thankfully, God does not disappear and then reappear as in the game with my children.

The scripture shown above refers to Hagar, the rejected handmaid of Sarai, the wife of Abraham. As she was being sent away from the camp in despair, Hagar *"saw"* and heard God speak to her, and yet she was amazed that *she didn't die.* Some of you may remember that when Moses (many years after Hagar's time) had an encounter with God at the burning bush on Mt. Sinai that he was not permitted to see God's face—it was only safe for him to see God's back as He walked before Moses (See Exodus 33:18-23 AMP).

God looked beyond time and saw Hagar's plight—and allowed her to "see" Him as He comforted her with news of a promising future for her and her son, Ishmael, even though they were ostracized from the house of his father, Abraham.

God also allows us to see Him spiritually, and sometimes in special physical ways, as He guides us through the cloudy veils of our most hurtful circumstances, times of uncertainty, and failures—and yet He also *permits us to live.*

So be alert and watch for Him—because
He is already watching out for us!

—Phyllis Andrews

Understanding

I am a big question-asker. Questions come to my mind all the time. Why? Because I want to know the answers. I want to understand. I am profoundly interested.

When I am in a one-on-one conversation with someone, I want to understand them; to hear what they're saying, and even more importantly to grasp the full meaning behind their words. The One I especially want to understand is the personal, loving, complex God who I worship. I want to know as much as He will allow me to know of Himself. If I understand His perspective on things that I face every day, and I will be so much better off and legitimately secure IF I align my thinking and behavior with His. I have the choice to do that or not. But first, I must be able to understand what His truth is.

My understanding of God comes in small chunks. I learn a bit about His character here and a dose of what He expects of me there. That seems to be the way God reveals Himself to most of us. This section contains my tidbits of understanding, along with those of three guest writers. We share this with you and pray that our wise God will give it the power and impact as He wills.

Nuggets of Understanding

"The beginning of wisdom is this: Get wisdom.
Though it cost all you have, get understanding."
Proverbs 4:7 (NIV)

Today, let's consider what it means to have understanding. Let's ponder these verses that are both nuggets *of* understanding and *about* understanding. Let them permeate and saturate your mind and heart:

"We know also that the Son of God has come
and has given us understanding,
so that we may know him who is true."
1 John 5:20 (NIV)

"Call to me, and I will answer you and tell you great
and unsearchable things you do not know."
Jeremiah 33:3 (NIV)

"A person may think their own ways are right,
but the Lord weighs the heart."
Proverbs 21:2 (NIV)

"…and if you call out for insight and cry aloud
for understanding, and if you look
for it as for silver and search for it as for hidden
treasure, then you will understand
the fear of the Lord and find the knowledge of God."
Proverbs 2:3-5 (NIV)

"So we fix our eyes not on what is seen, but on what is unseen.
For what is seen is temporary, but what is unseen is eternal."
2 Corinthians 4:18 (NIV)

"As the heavens are higher than the earth, so are my ways higher than
your ways and my thoughts than your thoughts."
Isaiah 55:9 (NIV)

"Do you not know? Have you not heard? The Lord is the everlasting God, the Creator of the ends of the earth. He will not grow tired or weary, and his understanding no one can fathom."
Isaiah 40:28 (NIV)

These verses tell us that God and his ways are knowable, yet at the same time, He is beyond a person's understanding. It's an interesting paradox, isn't it? But the more we seek His understanding, the more of it He will reveal! And one day, we'll know it all--in Heaven!

—Karen Furukawa

Perspective

"… how good is a timely word."
Proverbs 15:23 (NIV)

My 18-year old son and I were arguing again. I couldn't make him understand me. I needed him to grasp the importance of my point, but it appeared that he wasn't "getting it" at all—my son probably thought the same about me! What could I do but continue to persuade and convince him, talking it out until he "got it?" Finally, I gave up and went into another room to sit beside my husband.

My husband gently said to me, "You're not going to get through to him that way. You keep 'talking at him' and when he doesn't 'get it,' you 'talk at him' more. It would be better if you'd clearly make your point and *then back off.*"

You know, I understood immediately that my husband was right! His way was much more effective! That was precisely what I needed to hear at that moment. My *perspective* was changed, and my eyes opened. I was determined to rectify my approach to communicating with my son.

Scripture, also, offers examples of timely words saving a bad situation. In I Samuel 25:1-35 (NIV), David was enraged at a harsh man named Nabal and was intent on killing him. But Nabal's wife, Abigail, being a wise woman, urged David to withhold vengeance, not for Nabal's sake, but for David's own sake, to remain clean before the Lord. Seeing the wisdom of her words, David relented and spared Nabal's life. With this *new perspective*, David said to her, "May you be blessed for your good judgment and for keeping me from bloodshed this day…" (vs. 33.)

There may be times when our words may influence others in gaining a better perspective on a matter; one that is just, loving and wise. The Lord is our source of "true and reliable words" (Proverbs 22:21 NIV). Passing *His* words on to others, at just the right moment, may help guide them to God's truth.

Let me conclude with a friend's insightful words to me, "We must keep in mind that there is no timely word or right perspective outside of God. We are *His* mouthpiece. *He* gives the words and timing."

To that, I say—"AMEN"!

—Karen Furukawa

To the Very End

*"We want each of you to show this same diligence to the very end,
so that what you hope for may be fully realized."*
Hebrews 6:11 (NIV)

If the title on this page were ABIDING, would you have skipped over it and flipped to another page? I believe some people would. Why? Because it sounds old-fashioned. Some think of it as "old school." Many words are like that: stalwart, devout, resolute, earnest, staunch, indefatigable, dedicated, steadfast, ardent, zealous, and unceasing. Now think of these words in terms of a person's faith. They describe a hardy, sturdy, persevering kind of faith! In my opinion, there's nothing stodgy or rusty about that!

It's persistent and powerful! It's influential and admirable!
It is what Christ desires of His people TODAY!

Let's focus now on the attribute of ABIDING as it looked in the life of the late Ruth Bell Graham (wife of Billy Graham), as described by their daughter, Anne Graham Lotz. "As a teenager, my room was directly over Mother's. At night I'd see the lights from her room reflected on the trees outside my window. When I slipped downstairs to talk to her, I'd find her bent over her bed in prayer. It was useless waiting for her to rise because she'd be there hours on end, so I'd trudge back upstairs. No matter how early I awoke in the morning, I'd see those lights from her window once again reflected on the trees outside. But in the morning, when I tumbled downstairs, I'd find her seated at her desk, earnestly studying the fourteen translations of the Bible she spread around her.

*My mother chose to make abiding in Christ one of the priorities
of her life. It's the love relationship I saw she had with Christ
that created a thirst within me for a similar relationship with
Him—something I'm still pursuing more of to this day."*[17]

Do you think this is old fashioned? What I understand is that abiding in Christ to the very end is paramount in developing our love relationship with Him.

—Karen Furukawa

A Soft Power

"Let another praise you, and not your own mouth."
Proverbs 27:2 (NIV)

The early 20th-century evangelist and teacher, Oswald Chambers wrote, "Who are the people who have influenced us most? Certainly not the ones who thought they did, but those who did not have even the slightest idea that they were influencing us. In the Christian life, godly influence is never conscious of itself. If we are conscious of our influence, it ceases to have the genuine loveliness, which is characteristic of the touch of Jesus."[18]

Galatians 6:3 (NIV) says, "...if anyone thinks he is something when he is nothing, he deceives himself." The Message Bible states it more clearly, "Don't be impressed with yourself." Sadly, some individuals *do* appear impressed with themselves—speaking too much about *their* ministry and *their* service. It's essential that others are aware of each ministry they work in, the quantity of their witnessing that week, and how busy they are with one community service or another. Jesus taught, (Matthew 6) when we give or help someone in need—or when we serve in any capacity—we should do it in secret. Does this mean we must sneak around and make sure no one ever sees us when we serve? Not at all! It simply means we should do it quietly and unobtrusively, without fanfare. If we feel we must "toot our own horn," then our motive may be to impress people more than to serve the Lord sincerely.

"Self-praise" doesn't smell good, does it? Pastor and author, Chuck Swindoll writes, "Walk devotedly with God but don't try to look like it. Others will know it if you're genuinely God's man or woman."[19]

We all need to understand that God hates pride but loves humility. The most effective and influential Christians in my life, have been the ones who, when they are just themselves, are kind, gracious, seeking God, and doing their best to glorify Him; not out to impress anyone. They are humble and understated. They exude a pleasant fragrance and a soft power.

They are merely reflecting Jesus.

—Karen Furukawa

Tree-Of-Life Words

"The one who has knowledge uses words with restraint,
and whoever has understanding is even-tempered."
Proverbs 17:27 (NIV)

My mother is a woman of few words. She often wishes she were more talkative—not that she is always silent. She is conversational in an "other-centered" way. I once read that people fall into one of two categories—those who communicate, "Here I am!" and those who communicate, "There you are!" My mom is a "there-you-are!" kind of person. She focuses on you.

My mother has opinions, but she doesn't push them on others. Her opinions are prayerfully and biblically formed, and her spiritual beliefs are dearly held, but not dogmatically voiced. It is precisely because she does not parade her opinions that others sometimes seek them out. When she does say what she thinks, she does so thoughtfully and reasonably, and people realize that there is wisdom in her words. One person noted that when my mom speaks, others quiet down to listen.

We tend to think that we make ourselves heard by expressing our opinions frequently, loudly, or long-windedly. We like to make sure others understand our position along with all our reasons. We want to show others how much we know, when (as the adage says) we would do better to listen and show how much we care.

A few well-chosen words spoken quietly can persuade better than a thousand words at full volume. Those of us who have been at the receiving end of "many words at full volume" know that we are more receptive to "a few well-chosen words spoken quietly." I know I get lost in too many words, and my mind tunes out full volume.

In this current political climate of boastful claims, reactive tweets, and bluster, we see people with differing views trying to crush one another's arguments and sometimes crush one another personally as well.

Proverbs 15:4 (NIV) helps us to understand that our words
can either crush the spirit or be a tree of life.

I'd rather offer a tree of life. Wouldn't you?

—Sharon Rustia

Remnant

*"And God sent me before you to preserve for you a remnant on earth,
and to keep alive for you many survivors."*
Genesis 45:7 (ESV)

As an occasional quilter, I always save my fabric remnants—the scraps of fabric left over from previous sewing projects. I keep those bits of material because there is the potential for a lovely quilt to be fashioned from those scraps when all the pieces are sewn together in a well-planned design.

Throughout history, God has preserved a remnant also. He has protected and preserved a remnant of His people. The nation of Israel faced wars and endured many devastating events. Most of the people rebelled against God; many turned to idols. A small portion, however, remained loyal despite the tests, captivities, and persecution.

First Kings 19 tells us of the prophet Elijah, who believed he was the only one left who still followed God. But the Lord said to him, "Yet I reserve seven thousand in Israel—all whose knees have not bowed down to Baal [idol]…" (vs. 18, NKJV). So, Elijah was not as alone as he first thought. God had preserved a remnant.

Let's fast forward a few thousand years to today and consider this interesting statement: "The most blessed remnant is that of the true Church, the body of Christ. Jesus made it clear that this remnant would be small… *'Many'* will find the way to eternal destruction, but *'few'* will find the way to eternal life (Matthew 7:13-14 ESV). We who believe in Jesus Christ as our Lord and Savior can, with great peace, rest in the fact that we belong to the *remnant."* (Author unknown).

Did you get that? We, in the church today, must understand that we are part of God's remnant to proclaim the Gospel of Jesus Christ throughout the ages. Though hardships and persecution increase, let us hold firm and not fall away.

—Karen Furukawa

Willing to Dig?

"... and if you look for it as for silver and search for it as for hidden treasure,
then you will understand the fear of the Lord..."
Proverbs 2:4-5 (NIV)

Digging for precious gems has occupied many in my area for hundreds of years. Arizona's early native Americans found turquoise, quartz, and obsidian. Nearby, the legendary Tombstone was the home of a rich deposited silver mine. By 1881, due to an influx of miners, Tombstone had become the largest town in Arizona. Nowadays, however, the tiny town is a destination for tourists rather than prospectors, but mining in Arizona is not a thing of the past. They still dig gold, silver, zinc, and great amounts of copper out of this land for their desirability and value.

Delving into the Word of God is also profitable for finding treasures. The riches of Scripture will last for eternity, far surpassing anything earthly jewels can offer. Students of the Bible from the past and the present have dug hard and deep to find what they're after—the nuggets of wisdom and slabs of truth. There's no question that the many facets of godly understanding are all encased in God's Word, ready to be found. But how much are you and I willing to dig for them? Just surface-reading a passage in the Bible isn't enough. We must read and re-read it. We must look for its meaning and implications and ponder it until it crystallizes. If we ask ourselves pertinent questions from the passage, it will take us in many directions. If we follow where the veins lead, that's where we will find the rich insights. What was hidden, the Holy Spirit will reveal. We may suddenly see with amazing clarity things we have never seen in the Scriptures before.

Our wise God chose not to lay the mother lode out on the open surface where it takes no effort to find. How much would we value or care for it then? When He knows we yearn for it enough to search, seek, and dig for it—putting in the time and hard work to discover it, that's when He takes us to the place of finding and understanding it.

—Karen Furukawa

GOD'S TRUTH GIVES LIGHT
AND UNDERSTANDING

In Good Standing

*"If we confess our sins, he is faithful and just to forgive us our
sins and to cleanse us from all unrighteousness."*
1 John 1:9 (ESV)

I don't sleep well at night if my skin feels sticky. It's a quirk of mine. To combat it, I shower at night, but sometimes my feet get sticky again from walking around the house, so I wash my feet once more before getting into bed.

Interestingly, Jesus used this same scenario to convey a spiritual lesson to his disciples. He told them, "A person who has had a bath needs only to wash his feet, his whole body is clean. And you are clean..." John 13:10 (NIV). What did He mean?

Author and teacher, Anne Graham Lotz explains, "Once we have been to the cross for our 'complete bath' we are clean. Our every sin is washed away permanently." She continues, "But we still sin! Our feet get dirty again! So, every day, we come back to the cross, not for forgiveness since we are already forgiven, but to confess our sin and be cleansed that we might maintain a right fellowship with God."[20]

In Greek, the word "confess" means "to agree with." If we confess our sin, we agree with God that we have wronged Him. So, let's confess! Let's assume responsibility for our wrongdoing instead of dodging it or blaming others. Doesn't every parent yearn for this from his or her child? So does our Abba Father! Once we've confessed our sin to Him, every hindrance is removed, and the sweet, full fellowship returns!

Yes, I might wash my feet before getting into bed at night, but I understand, that matters not!

Daily confessing my sin to God, which keeps me in good
standing with Him—now that *does* matter!

—Karen Furukawa

See

"Taste and see that the Lord is good…"
Psalm 34:8 (NIV)

I have lived in Arizona since the age of two before finally seeing the Grand Canyon just a few years ago. A common sentiment among those who had seen this world wonder was that pictures do not do it justice. I would not know its true awesomeness or feel the same sense of wonder until I had seen it for myself.

I once went on a mission's trip to Jamaica. We were working at a children's home that sits at the top of the Blue Mountains. I will never forget the refreshing mountain air, crisp and pure. Birds of Paradise, ferns, Hibiscus and other unfamiliar tropical flowers lined the mountain's ledge. Beyond was the city of Kingston, and beyond that, the ocean. The colors of water and sky blended in the distance, making it hard to tell where the water ended and the sky began. Each evening, billowing clouds would roll in, and the sky was set ablaze with a radiant sunset. Unless you have made the winding fourteen-mile trek up that mountain, you can never fully know what I mean despite my best attempt at describing it. You must see it for yourself.

I feel the same way about God and grace. I wish I could paint with words in a way that you can see and understand who He is. But words are not enough. A person cannot fully know the beauty and feel the awe of who God is unless they have experienced Him for themselves. I want others to know grace for more than just a word. If you don't know God, can I invite you to *"taste and see that the Lord is good?"* If you have not experienced His grace, can I invite you to come a little closer and get to know Him better? And when you have, then you will understand this awe and this love that I feel for an amazing God. Then you will see exactly what I mean.

—Olivia Brant

The Right Hand of God

"...I will strengthen you, I will help you; I will uphold
you with my victorious right hand."
Isaiah 41:10 (RSV)

The sharp visual image of the right hand represents several great principles of our nation. Our right hand placed over our heart expresses devotion to our flag and country. A right-hand salute in the Armed Forces conveys honor and respect to persons of a higher rank. The right hand lifted or placed upon a Bible while taking an oath in a court of law promises one's commitment, to telling the truth.

Similarly, the imagery of God's right hand in the Bible signifies greatness also. The Old Testament speaks of God's right hand as glorious and victorious, as full of power and strength. His mighty right hand sustained, saved, helped, upheld, strengthened, and brought victory to His people.

In the New Testament, the focus of God's right-hand changes; a new dimension is added. Here, the right hand of God almost exclusively refers to the honored and exalted position in heaven where Jesus, the Messiah sits. He resides at the right hand of the Father, and do you know what He is doing there? Do you understand that He is interceding for us (See Hebrews 7:25 - RSV)? Do you understand that He is forgiving sins (See Acts 5:31- RSV), and that He is ruling (See 1 Peter 3:22 - RSV)?

My heart responds to the implications of the right hand of God. Whatever circumstance I may find myself in, I can rely on God's strong right hand to sustain and uphold me. I am comforted knowing that Jesus is *now* at the right hand of the Father, ruling, forgiving *my* sins, and interceding for *me*. He is not merely sitting on high—distant and uncaring. Just the opposite! He is directly involved with me—and you!

—Karen Furukawa

Mary Understood Differently

"Then Mary took a twelve-ounce jar of expensive perfume made
from the essence of nard, and she anointed Jesus' feet with it,
wiping his feet with her hair. The house was filled with the fragrance."
John 12:3 (NLT)

Mary of Bethany understood differently. She hadn't scurried around the kitchen with her sister, Martha. She took the time to enjoy Jesus' company when He visited them. Jesus said it was the most appropriate response to Him that day. She had overwhelming joy and gratitude at her brother, Lazarus' supernatural resurrection from the dead by Jesus, and their lives were restored all because of Him. The siblings and followers all loved Jesus deeply, but Mary understood differently.

The last mention of Mary shows her to have become a woman of thoughtful and worshipful action. She knew Passover was near and Jesus had spoken of his burial. Mary, at Jesus' feet, must have understood, even better than the disciples, that Jesus was going to die. She poured out expensive perfumed oil on Jesus' feet then gently wiped his feet with the oil-soaked locks of her hair. Judas, the betrayer's "piety" was shocked and maybe even embarrassed by Mary's profoundly intimate and lavish expression of love for her Lord. But Mary of Bethany understood differently.

Jesus connected Mary's anointing and his burial in John 12:7 (NLT). Mary had kept the unique anointing perfume in her possession for the very purpose she had intended—to announce the nearness of Jesus' death and prepare for His burial. She understood that the pleasant perfume was a screaming contrast to Jesus' death and burial. She understood that she was not anointing Jesus as [a] king or Messiah. She was anointing him as a corpse. A beautiful scent and an ugly crucifixion seem incompatible, but the Apostle John tells us in 12:32 (NLT) that Jesus is lifted on a cross that He might attract all to Himself.

Mary's example permits us also to honor Jesus in extravagant, unorthodox ways. Jesus receives our affection, too, as part of our devotion to Him in the giving of our whole selves to Him.

Mary of Bethany sat at His feet. And she understood.

—Pat Olson

May His Face Shine Upon You

"...the Lord make His face shine upon you and be gracious to you;"
Numbers 6:25 (NIV)

One day in junior high school, my sister Sharon, stood outside her school building chatting with two other girls. These two girls had recently started experimenting with cigarettes, so on this occasion, they pulled out their matches and cigarettes and proceeded to smoke. They asked Sharon to join them. Sharon was uncomfortable but considered trying it because she was curious about what it was like to smoke. She also felt pressure to go along with them, to conform. Sharon was tempted to give in—but she found she couldn't do it! Something held her back.

Sharon explained to me later, saying, "I pictured Mom's sweet face and how disappointed she would look when she found out I smoked, and I just couldn't hurt her that way." Sharon's love for Mom overcame her temptation and pressure to smoke. She understood that her respect for Mom outweighed the opinions of her friends. Bringing pain to Mom is something Sharon refused to do.

Isn't that beautiful? And isn't that the way we should be with God? Shouldn't our love for Him be so tender and real that we can't bear to grieve Him? (See Ephesians 4:30 - NIV). Shouldn't our respect and indebtedness to Him cause us to keep ourselves aligned with Him? (See Romans 12:2 - NIV). Shouldn't we be faithful to Him because He was first faithful to us (See Hebrews 10:23 - NIV)?

So, the next time you face temptation, what will you do? Will you do just as you please? Or will you remember the One who loves you and live to please Him? Will His countenance be shadowed with grief by your choices? Or will you act in a way that will "make His face shine upon you" because of your faithfulness?

I hope you will know the favor and blessing of
His face shining upon you.

—Karen Furukawa

Our Enemy

"so that we would not be outwitted by Satan; for
we are not ignorant of his designs."
2 Corinthians 2:11 (ESV)

In this world, we fight daily battles against an expert tactician—Satan. The Bible identifies him as our enemy. He is not just a myth or a symbol of evil. He is real, and he hates everyone, especially Christians.

We all realize that Satan purposely disrupts our lives with intense attacks that cause immense fear, pain, and suffering. Most often though, I believe his tactic is to manipulate us in quiet ways through stealthy deceptions, half-truths, and subtle temptations. He schemes to catch us unaware. He attempts to side-track us from God's purposes by convincing us that we need to fill our time and energy on busy work. That appears to be "a good thing," but it isn't what God wants—Satan stealing our time and focus. Another of his furtive tactics is to get us to compare ourselves with others. Then he is instantly successful because either we'll become discouraged or we'll get puffed-up, depending on how we feel we measure-up next to "the other guy." Both outcomes give Satan the victory!

Scripture refers to Satan as "the accuser" (See Revelation 12:10 - ESV). Author, John Eldredge, explains that Satan puts accusing thoughts in our minds, like "You're such a poser" or "You don't have anything worthwhile to say," causing us to hate ourselves. Even worse, Satan desires us to hate God. Eldredge writes, "Satan...leaps to accuse God in our hearts that God isn't *really* out for our best, or that if God were *really* loving He would make things smoother for us."[21]

We must understand that we cannot allow Satan to fool us. We must never believe his lies. Remember, Satan is cunning. We must always be on the lookout for his ploys, tricks, or traps.

—Karen Furukawa

Change

"See, I am doing a new thing! Now it springs up;
do you not perceive it? I am making a way..."
Isaiah 43:19 (NIV)

Have you heard the saying, "Change equals stress"? Most of us dislike change because it upsets our routines and threatens our comfort level. It leaves us feeling insecure. No one likes feeling that way.

With my husband in the military, he and I moved repeatedly. We uprooted our children and household, again and again, to relocate to the next assignment in another state or another country. We moved ahead into the unknown, to the unfamiliar and started anew. Do you think all that change caused stress? Yes, it certainly did! Now I want to let you know something else—the Lord enabled me to learn this lesson. I came to understand that if I focus on a positive aspect of moving, it will buffer the negative part. What positive aspect of moving did I find? Just this—poking around and getting to know our new locale is fun! Exploring the new region and discovering the distinct color, flavor, and beauty of the place is an adventure! I love that part of moving now!

Are you caught in a situation? Are you in the midst of stressful change? Ask the Lord to show you at least one positive thing you can focus on or one opportunity open to you that will lift you.

My husband retired from the military a few years ago, and we've happily remained in our current home for nine grateful years. It now appears that another move with all the changes and stress that accompanies it might again be on our horizon. If so, I hope to take Isaiah 43:19 to heart. I aspire to see this move, this change as from the Lord—doing a new thing in our lives, something positive and according to His plan. As Isaiah says," [He] will make a way" amid the stresses, the questions, and difficulties. He will make a way!

—Karen Furukawa

Found

I'm forty years old on one side. If you're good at math, you'll know that I've lived a long time—twenty-nine wonderful years in Arizona.

I decided to write my autobiography—776 pages. Until that time, I couldn't write a good grocery list. God is faithful and would never encourage me to do something without giving me all I needed to complete the task. I like to keep writing light and to the point. I hope you enjoy my collections on the word, FOUND. All that to say, I found what God was prompting me to write.

The Absence of Sound

*"Don't worry about anything; instead, pray about everything;
tell God your needs, and don't forget to thank him for his answers."*
Philippians 4:6 (TLB)

Have you ever lost something of value--Something that may not seem like a big deal to someone else, but to you it seems like everything?

That's what happened to me recently. I lost my voice. Why I don't know—it just happened. One minute I was sitting on the back porch verbalizing with the Lord and the next—there was nothing. It was the strangest thing. It had never happened before, nor ever since. It was a shock!

My mind took over, searching—why, why? In the absence of sound, I found the answer. This time I felt God was speaking:

*Listen and be still. Take this time to appreciate the absence of sound silently.
Take a minute to throw your cares on me. Hold all the gifts that I've given
you in your thoughts and heart. If you do this, I will bless your every
utterance from this time forward. Speak as if I am speaking through you.
You will receive your speech and when you do,
speak for Me, your Lord and Savior,
and then don't forget to thank Me.*

—Audrey Rierson

Great Artisan

"… declares the LORD. *"Like clay in the hand of the potter,*
so are you in my hand…"
Jeremiah 18:6 (NIV)

We are all aware of the stories of the potter, who was not satisfied with his creation. He would toss it back on the pottery wheel and start over again. It is a simple process to be able to work a piece of art until it's exactly what the potter had in mind.

Not so, when we examine the specific art of forming iron sculpture. A lot of care and patience must be given to melt, bend, and change the metal. To produce a piece of sculpture, you must start with a foundry—a place where metal is cast in molds under high heat. Different metals produce different strengths and textures. Too much of one metal can make a product that will bend, and another will harden it to the max. Every melted composite has a specific function to do for that creation. The metallurgist must know how hot to make the furnace fire, when to melt the iron, and when to add the components to the exact specifications. As the molten iron is poured into a mold, the artist must be aware of the heat that is being handled. If he lets it cool down, it won't pour properly, and the art piece will have holes and pockmarks. If the lava flows at the perfect temperature and angle into the mold, it will become the piece of art the ironmaster desired from the beginning. In other words, a piece fit for a king.

Throughout our lives, we've been formed like clay on a wheel with all the mastery of a potter. At times, our Potter has taken our lump, smacked, and reformed it. We need to be molded into something of strength and beauty. Our great Artisan, God, knew how hot to make our melting process to mold us toward the perfect pattern of Jesus.

In my life, I have found that God wants our
form to be what He desires us to be.

—Audrey Rierson

Perfectly Planned

*"And a man of the house of Levi went and took
as wife a daughter of Levi. So the
woman conceived and bore a son. And when she saw that he was a beautiful
child, she hid him three months. But when she
could no longer hide him, she took
an ark of bulrushes for him, daubed it with asphalt and pitch, put the child
in it, and laid it in the reeds by the river's bank. And his sister
stood afar off, to know what would be done to him."*
Exodus 2:1-4 (NKJV)

Many of us know the Bible story of a Hebrew man and woman, who FOUND themselves pregnant during the time when Pharaoh was allowing only Hebrew girls to be born and grow to maturity. God arranged circumstances concerning the birth of their special male child. His mother decided to hide him and hopefully grow him to maturity, escaping the death threat of Pharaoh. After a while it became harder to keep him out of sight, so his mother wove a little basket out of river reeds and tar and placed him in it.

His family lived along the Nile River, which flowed past the palace of Pharaoh. Pharaoh's daughter came to the river to bathe and spotted a little container entwined in the reeds. She asked one of her friends to get it. A beautiful baby boy, unharmed and safe, was found. Pharaoh's daughter held the baby and knew that he must have nourishment. One of the women asked the princess if she would like her to find a Hebrew woman, who could nurse the baby. The princess agreed. The women, who were to summon the mother was none other than the baby's sister. The princess met with the women, and she agreed to nurse and care for him. But the tale just gets started here with the punch line—"they named him Moses" (See Exodus 2:10 – NKJV).

What were the chances that the princess would find a little basket on the edge of the river? What were the chances that the baby's boat wouldn't spring a leak? What were the chances that the baby's sister was able to watch and then be summoned by the daughter of Pharaoh to bring back none other than the baby's mother? These were not random circumstances, but a perfect plan that was divinely timed and arranged by God.

Let's compare that with each of us who have found ourselves floating along in a river with nothing to do, except coast along with the tide of our circumstances. Then at some point, we were plucked up and saved by divine timing.

Whatever the circumstances, your little ark eventually rested in the arms of a loving Father and all in His timing. If we are willing, we can go with the flow and accept the conditions that will allow us to have a life of blessings, and conquer anything put before us, just like baby Moses.

—Audrey Rierson

Possible or Impossible?

"Do not forget to entertain strangers, for by so doing some have unwittingly entertained angels."
Hebrews 13:2 (NKJV)

I was lost but now I'm found.

It happened about ten years ago on an Indian Reservation in Arizona. My husband and I heard of a little lake on the reservation teeming with fish. We stopped at the Indian National Tourist Office and were greeted at the door by a young, attractive woman, who wore the most beautiful turquoise jewelry. Her sweet smile invited us in. The trophies of deer, bear, red fox, a beautiful rainbow trout and more fill the office.

We asked for information about a little-known lake, called Takalai. The young lady smiled, pointed to the enormous rainbow, and said, "That came out of Lake Takalai." Boy, did that get the adrenalin going!

We asked, "So where is this lake?" It appeared there were two ways to get there—the easier way had a small landslide; the shortest route was a "bit rough," it had hardly any vehicle traffic and was very narrow. We decided to take the narrow path. We were ready for a rainbow trout dinner!

We paid for our Indian fishing license—a small price to pay for fresh trout—and started on our way.

We found the road! The scenery was magnificent, but no lake in sight. We had driven over ten miles; it didn't seem right because we had not seen another car. Our minds started to wonder—could this be an Indian ambush? We ran out of "path" and stopped. We were trapped! In plain English—we were lost! There were no houses or any other sign of habitation. We opened our truck doors, forcing them to break mesquite branches. We thought we could make a three-point turn, but that was impossible.

Coming back around the back of the truck, we saw a big rock about three feet high with an old Indian sitting on it! Yes, you read, right. There was an Indian in the middle of nowhere.

I was speechless, but my husband found words. He said, "What are you doing here?"

"Resting!" was his gravelly voice reply, followed by, "What are YOU doing here?

"We're looking for the Lake," we replied.

"Well, you won't find it from here. You should have stayed on the road to the left. You veered off to the right".

"But, what do we do now?" I asked.

"Come and follow me." We looked at each other—got in the truck and drove until we came to a spot for a perfect three-point turn.

We pulled in, made the turn, stopped, and pulled down the tailgate. We were ready for a cold soda. We offered our Indian friend a Dr. Pepper—he was very grateful for it.

He didn't say much except thanks as he hopped off the tailgate. We asked if we could give him a ride to "somewhere," but he said, "No, thanks."

As we headed out, I saw no trace of him in the rear-view mirror. He vanished! The question was, did we find him, or did he find us? We could say that we found each other, which led to the next question. Was he an angel?

Heading home, we knew our Lord was with us that day, making the impossible, possible—with nothing more than a few scratches on our truck and an unforgettable story.

That evening we found a Denny's and enjoyed a delicious fish dinner.

—Audrey Rierson

Christmas Box

"Now eagerly desire the greater gifts."
1 Corinthians 12:31 (NIV)

It was all Marilyn wanted for Christmas. One of her little friends had received a "birthstone" ring for her birthday. Marilyn didn't know why, but she thought that was the most special thing anyone could ever own.

Her mom and dad lived on a very tight budget so Christmas presents would be sparse, but it would be worth asking for a birthstone ring. The look her parents gave her told her she could expect socks and underwear.

The tree was put up in the living room, just as in years past. A small box under the tree would look good, but it wasn't meant to be.

Christmas Eve found four beautifully wrapped boxes. Two for her brother and two for her. Her brother's box looked to contain a truck or toy and the other, you guessed it underwear and socks. Marilyn's boxes were a puzzlement—the one was, no doubt about it, underwear and socks, but the other one was huge, about twenty inches square.

It was time for the walk to church for Midnight Mass. The church was decorated beautifully, and the organist played the Christmas hymns.

Even with all the ceremony and candle lights, Marilyn found it hard to concentrate. All she could think of was that huge box. A gentle snow was falling on the way home. She turned to her mom and asked could she open presents on Christmas Eve. It was late, and it wasn't a good idea mom said, so off to bed.

She slid into bed, but she found she couldn't sleep. The box was all she could envision as she closed her eyes. "God, this doesn't look good, please, the ring," she said.

It was morning—time to open presents. Marilyn ran down the hall to see the gifts. Mom slid the big box over, addressed, "To our sweet precious, Marilyn. We love you so much!"

She ripped off the paper, finding an ordinary cardboard box—inside was a box within another box with an advertisement for four gallons of laundry soap. Confused, she heard mom say, "Well, open it!" She ripped this box open and found a shoe box after unfolding this wrapping, another box, a "Pop-Tart" box. Her brother encouraged her to open it! There inside of the small box was a little black box. Everyone watched her expression, as she opened the box. She couldn't believe it! There it was! The most beautiful birthstone ring ever.

Our lives are similar. It takes the act of peeling off our sinful layers to get to the gifts—He has for us. The only gift that matters is your relationship with Jesus.

—Audrey Rierson

God's Covenant

"But Noah found favor in the eyes of the Lord."
Genesis 6:8 (NIV)

After the failure of Adam and Eve of the Bible, you can only imagine how hurt God was—from a human point of view, that is. He had given His creation everything good in the world and they blew it. It must have grieved Him in His heart.

I can hear the God of heaven and earth contemplate destroying all the wonders He had made.

We can only imagine how Noah of the Old Testament was jeered, cursed, and called insane. In obedience to God, he carried out the task that was put before him until he completed it. Noah was 600 years old when the flood water was on the earth.

Noah found the strength that could only come from a loving God. In his mercy, God established a covenant with him for perpetual generations. The covenant can still be seen today as a reminder to us that God will never destroy the earth again with water. A rainbow—an excellent reminder that God is a forgiving God.

It's almost impossible for us to conceive that God could forgive us, but under the new covenant, God sent His Son, Jesus to live and die for our sins. The flood of the precious blood that flowed from Jesus' side can wash us clean.

Now it's our turn. All we must do is accept that sacrifice and invite Jesus into our lives.

—Audrey Rierson

The Wonderful Pacifier

"He calms the storm and stills the waves. What a blessing
is that stillness, as He brings them safely into harbor!"
Psalm 107:29 (TLB)

Mom and Dad have just brought their newborn baby home from the hospital. The nursery had been set up two weeks before and everything was perfect. Baby was placed in the crib as mom and dad proudly observed every breath and slight smile of their newborn infant. So peaceful and serene. While mom was exhausted, dad was filled with the realization that this was real. The feeling of great responsibility came over him as he sat beside his wife, trying to feel like the father figure, the man in charge.

A few hours passed, and then a slight whimper was heard. The two of them jumped to their feet and picked the darling baby up in their arms, with a look of, "what do we do now?"

"Baby needs to be fed," both said in unison. That's a job for Mom, so Dad was off the hook for the time being.

Baby is then fed and now needs changing. "Okay, we can handle this. That's not so bad." Mom and dad took turns handling and caressing baby. It is time for another catnap.

It's time for them to have a light supper. "Listen, baby's crying again. Mom, that's your signal." They questioned—does this go on every four hours?

Let's fast forward to three weeks into family life. Mom and Dad are beat, and the baby is crying a lot more between feedings. Enter Aunt Sue.

Auntie comments on the amount of crying, while Mom and Dad nod— they're too tired to respond. Aunt Sue suggests, "What you need darlin' is a pacifier. I'll go to the store and get one".

Pacifier in hand, Aunt Sue runs it under hot water to sterilize it—baby is instantly quiet as he sucks on a new-found friend. It worked! What a wonderful thing! From that time forward, that wonderful invention would never leave the baby's side until—baby's most important accessory is missing.

"Who saw it last? Dad, where is it? Mom, where did you leave it?" All they know is baby is not happy. Pick baby up, rock baby, feed the baby. But it's not time—where is that pacifier?

The last time I saw it was right here. Well, it isn't there now! I am! I'm going to feed the baby, and I don't care if it's not time. Baby won't stop crying. Baby isn't hungry. Baby wants that thing and won't stop crying until he gets it. Try changing! The diaper is dry. Where is that 'cotton picken' pacifier? Look in the living room. I did! Look in our bedroom, I did! Look under the crib! I found it! Under the crib. Without thinking twice, that (dirty) pacifier went right into baby's tiny lips—and all was quiet.

Just like us in some ways, we scream and cry for something that can help us when we're in torment when all we need is Jesus to calm our spirit and release our yearning. Let Jesus be the pacifier in your life to calm your spirit and appease your soul's longing. He can do it, all you must do is ask, and you'll find peace in Jesus.

—Audrey Rierson

A CALM SPIRIT IS FOUND IN JESUS

Food for The Soul

"For Jehovah hears the cries of His needy ones
and does not look the other way."
Psalm 69:33 (TLB)

Hey over here, look what I found.

"Be careful, Carlos, you'll slip and fall, and we won't get you out. "Here, it was worth it, a whole bag of apples. This one isn't so bad; I can get five good bites off it."

That was the scene at a dump in Santa Maria, Mexico, about ten years ago at Ranchito de Cristo Mission.

Jenny, the missionary, and I packed a pickup truck with clothes, shoes, toys, and food. Lots of food! We went down paths with potholes as big as the truck. The first time I went, I thought Jenny was lost. In front of us was a massive pile of garbage, and the stench was horrible. Jenny said, "This is our stop!"

"Here?" I asked.

"Let's just get out, and you'll see." We jumped out of the truck and started walking to the back. At least thirty-five children came running towards the truck, all smiles. They were dirty, scratched, but they had the most beautiful smiles. They hugged us and spoke in Spanish, so I didn't know what they were saying exactly, but I knew without a doubt, they were happy to see Jenny.

We started handing out shoes first. Then five big boxes of clothing. They didn't care if it was the right size or color. To them, they fit perfectly. Some took their old clothes off right away; others clutched the "new" T-shirts as if they were gold. Others asked for clothes for a brother or sister. They stood waiting because they knew what was coming next—FOOD! Jenny told everyone to form a line. We started unloading produce. Everyone got a bunch of carrots that they started eating right away. Then the various fruit was distributed.

They were asked to sit by a tree in the shade—where the best food was shared—the Word of God. We spoke, and a few children chimed in. We found several little evangelists. I could have sat there for hours as we all shared. It's odd—the waft of smelly garbage was hardly noticeable. We sang a few songs and listened to their stories. Those two hours seemed like a few minutes.

As we left everyone came to get a hug. Jenny said, "Wait a minute," and motioned for me to get the last two boxes. The kids sat back down as if on cue. I brought out the boxes, and the smiles said it all. Only one word on the box– "Hershey's!" We gave each child a candy bar and a children's Bible. They were told to tell their parents what they learned about Jesus, and with that, they left, plastic bag in hand. We were so glad that we found them before they had eaten rotten garbage—they'll be back again soon.

They may be poor and hungry, but they received food that will last forever—nourishing words from the Bible. We pray that they live a life in Jesus, so that they may be found at the "banquet table" in heaven.

—Audrey Rierson

Arizona Sunset

"You will find me when you seek me, if you look for me in earnest."
Jeremiah 29:13 (TLB)

While on a recent trip east of the Mississippi River, I found a totally different landscape.

My home in Arizona—is situated in what they call high desert. You'll find valleys, mountains, plains, and plateaus. Some places allow you to see forever, while other areas are canyons with towering walls. There is almost always a gorgeous sunset at the end of the day—helping you calm down and unwind for a relaxing evening.

In the East, there are towering mountains, called skyscrapers—mountains made of steel and glass. Their valleys are the neighborhoods winding through the cities. The valleys are usually dark because of the shade created by large buildings. When the sun starts to go down, it shines on the glass structures in a reflection of blinding light. I wonder how many people living in these cities have seen a sunset that is not marred by man's creation. It seems that the hustle and bustle of the day are trapped between the structures without an opportunity to calm down, relax, and prepare for the night.

For me, that is the time when our Lord and I talk. There's so much happening during the day—distractions, appointments, and chores. The half-hour that allows for sunset is the best time for a connection. I can tell Him [Lord] about my day. If I listen carefully, He tells me how to fix the problems and encourages me to try a different solution.

As we converse, He's got me ready for the new day He has in store for me. I don't know if it could be the same with a different set of brick and mortar. Maybe it's possible, but frankly, I don't want to find out.

God has planted me, and I wouldn't change. Wherever you find yourself in the world at the end of the day, try to make it a quiet space to communicate with the One that made it all possible—the God of the universe, and the creator of beautiful sunsets.

—Audrey Rierson

Best Gift Ever

"You search the Scriptures, for in them you think
you have eternal life; and these are they which testify of Me."
John 5:39 (NKJV)

Christmas is a wonderful time of year—it's a time full of surprises, goodies, and visits from relatives. It's a time when six-year-olds get excited. In 1966 my son, Sam, was asking, no begging for a two-wheeled bike. With three other children also wanting extravagant presents we were not able to stretch a budget.

My parents were visiting that Christmas and inquired what the kids asked Santa for. I explained that the only request was for two-wheeled bikes. My dad laughed and said that would be Sam's request! They would buy a bike and some other special gifts for the other children.

With all the children still in school, we went to work. My dad went out to his car and brought in a large box holding "the bike." He placed it against the wall while mom spread a red tablecloth over the box. Then dad said, "let's put up the tree" and mom started unwrapping each statue of the manger scene, placing each in precisely where they have stood for every Christmas for as long as I could remember.

The school bus was coming, and we all rushed to get presents from the trunk of their car. They greeted Grandma and Grandpa as their eyes glance to the packages and boxes under the tree.

Then it hit Sam, "Mom," he said, I can't find any box that would be big enough for a two-wheeled bike." My only answer was, "you'll just have to wait and see."

Finally, it was Christmas Eve. We all gathered around the tree and Nativity display. They gave each one a present. Three children were happy with their gifts, but not Sam. He set aside the box that contained the set of Matchbox cars. The race car track got a slight response, but we could see it didn't quench the desire for a two-wheeled bike.

After the presents were opened, tears started to well up in Sam's eyes. He moved closer to grandpa and said, "I wanted a bike, grandpa. Just then grandma asked Sam to come over to the manger. Grandma gently unpinned the red tablecloth and lifted the scene to expose a box with big red letters spelling out, "Schwinn." Sam didn't know what to say or do. At least ten thank you's were heard as Grandpa completely unwrapped the box. They placed the manger on the coffee table as grandpa, dad and Sam started putting the bike together.

Now, as a Christian, I see a sidebar to this story. Sometimes when we are searching for something and not finding it, it could be leading us to Jesus. When we find Him, it's the best gift we can receive.

—Audrey Rierson

A Life Well Lived

"I strain to reach the end of the race and receive
the prize for which God is calling us
up to heaven because of what Christ Jesus did for us."
Philippians 3:14 (TLB)

My dad was the healthiest man I've ever known. He didn't believe in doctors but would use his parents old home remedies.

My parents lived in an apartment above a funeral home. After my father retired, he assisted the undertaker with his duties.

It was December 18, 1972, and my whole family was Christmas shopping. We got home at about 8:00 p.m.

The phone was ringing. I answered. It was the funeral home director with a simple statement that no daughter wants to hear. He said four words, "Your dad is dead."

"No, that's impossible," I said, "no, no, no."

"He died at 1:30 this afternoon. Your mother has seen a doctor and is resting comfortably. There's no reason for you to come this evening. My wife will stay with her through the night."

I set my family down to try to tell them the news. Four children could not believe the news—"Grandpa is gone." My husband and I tried to keep our composure, but we failed. The tears came.

When I arrived, my mom was in shock. We cried together for as long as it took to compose ourselves. Just then, the director knocked and came in. "I thought you'd want to know what exactly happened," he said. "Part of your Dad's job was to pick up the mail around noon for our business. Yesterday was no exception."

It seems Dad went to get the mail as usual and never came back. Dad reached for the mail with his foot in the door. The apparent massive heart attack killed him halfway in and halfway outside the door—he was found in that position.

In my opinion, Dad had the best of both worlds. He lived a very healthy life and died a quick death—no feeble mind, no daily handful of pills, no wheelchair, and no endless therapy. Just a life well lived when Jesus' took him home in an instant.

Here's the important thing we can learn from this story. You never know when or where the Lord will call you home. If you dedicate your life to Jesus, you have nothing to worry about. In that split second that phenomenal act happens—there's no thinking through anything.

If you haven't received salvation through Jesus Christ, you might want to think about that now, while you still have time. You might want to think about where you'll be found taking your last breath on earth.

—Audrey Rierson

Divine Commitment

"I knew you before you were formed within your mother's womb; before you were born, I sanctified you and appointed you as my spokesman to the world."
Jeremiah 1:5 (TLB)

I was an only child, but I had 15 cousins. Growing up I was very close to two male cousins who were older. We had fun and tried to stay out of trouble—(WE TRIED.)

With these cousins came five aunties, the best ladies you can imagine. Our get-to-gathers were always, "over the top."

My two cousins became "my big brothers." We got closer as the years progressed. The aunties got older and passed away, so getting any family history from the "older" generation became nearly impossible. If I needed an old special recipe, there was no one to call. If I needed an auntie for help with a crocheted stitch—no one.

We all start getting older, and memories begin to fade in our close family. "Do you remember the time we …?" "What was the name of that…?" It seemed that the memories were fading fast. My "big brother" cousins and I sat down at dinner and talked. I did the prodding, and they searched their brains. I had a lot of information, but *what was I going to do with it?*

Although I couldn't put a grocery list together, I decided to write my life's story. I didn't know what I was getting into when I started, but I felt I was on a mission. Who better to write about me, then me? I looked at old pictures to bring back memories and gather stories. The best thing I did was pray. My two "big brothers" called every once in an awhile to see "how it was going." We laughed and reminisced.

I didn't know how to write a book, but this is the way I did it. I would get up early, eat breakfast, clean my kitchen, shop, work in the garden—all before noon. Any given day was different, but that was the plan I adopted. I'd have a light lunch and then start to pray over my computer, "Lord, you know I don't have a clue on how to write an autobiography, so please help me every step of the way." After prayer, I'd write from 1:00 until 4:00. Every day the same time frame, basically the same prayer! Sure, some things came up to change my plan, but I always tried to stick to it.

So now to the end of my story. I was so happy that I found time to commit to finishing my book. Otherwise, I doubt if I would have finished a 776-page book, "He Was Always There" © 2018. The happy ending was exciting. One of my big brothers had my book read to him in the hospital as his health was fading. Two days after closing the cover, he passed away.

If God sets up a circumstance in your life and all the pieces come together, take hold of it and you will find time to pursue it. You'll be blessed, and you might bless others.

—Audrey Rierson

The Prayer Diet

*"For in Christ there is all of God in a human body; so,
you have everything when you have Christ, and you are
filled with God through your union with Christ."*
Colossians 2:9,10 (TLB)

Right after Christmas I suppose everyone goes on a diet—well at least my friends do. It seems the pounds start to add up the day after that big Thanksgiving dinner. But then a short month later, we find ourselves attending family get-togethers and office parties, not to mention church potlucks and neighborhood fellowships. All, that to say, it seems impossible to stay on a diet or simply refuse food at these parties.

So, on and on it goes until the end of January when we can't get our zipper zipped. Then, out come the loose-fitting tops and the elastic waist slacks. I know you're smiling now because you know it's true. After a few days, you decide you must go on a diet. You call your friend (a good friend) to let her in on your plan. She's determined to do the same and suggests we go on a diet together. We'll check up on each other to report our progress and compliment when appropriate and chastise when needed.

And so, it was. The first week, neither of us had any good news to report. It was slow going. We both would keep on starving if that's what it took to lose a few pounds.

The weeks went on, and I was starving and thought, at this point, my bathroom scale, must be stuck. No results. I started gaining weight. How could that be? In my mind, I was as skinny as a rail by now, but the scale told a whole different story.

"Miss skinny pants" called proudly saying she had lost ten pounds and felt like a new person. She had to buy new jeans and tops." "Well," I said, "I have a whole new wardrobe too because I found the ten pounds that you lost!"

Do you think God minds how we look, how much we weigh, and what we eat? Think about it. God made us in His image and likeness. We owe it to God to keep ourselves as healthy as possible so we can honor Him with our bodies.

Yes, I did stick to it, and I did lose the pounds I "found," plus the original weight I meant to lose in the first place. It was hard but so rewarding. I did it with a focus on prayer. If you get the temptation for a second helping, pray the edge away. It works!

I want to say I found a NEW diet, the prayer diet. Try it!

—Audrey Rierson

What Would You Do?

"...Don't be afraid!" he said. "I bring you the most joyful news ever announced, and it is for everyone! The Savior—yes, the Messiah, the Lord—has been born tonight in Bethlehem! How will you recognize him? You will find a baby wrapped in a blanket, lying in a manger!"
Luke 2:10-12 (TLB)

There were shepherds in a field outside a small village guarding their flocks of sheep. They became very alarmed when an angel appeared. "Don't be afraid!" he said. "I bring you the most joyful news ever announced, and it is for everyone! The Savior—yes, the Messiah, the Lord—has been born tonight in Bethlehem!" The angel also told them that the baby would be found in a manger wrapped in a blanket.

After the angels left them, the shepherds said one to another, *"Come on! Let's go to Bethlehem! Let's see this wonderful thing that has happened, which the Lord has told us about "* (Luke 2:16 (TLB). It might be important to note that they ran to the village and found Mary, Joseph, and the baby lying in a manger just as the angel told them. They were astonished! The Savior, who they were told about all their lives, was there.

What would you have done if you found yourself before the newborn King? I wonder if I would be so bold as to ask Mary, "Please, may I hold Him? I'll be gentle!" If Mary had given permission, I would have felt like the most blessed person on earth. I would have felt so privileged to see the promised Messiah.

Like the shepherds, we too can herald the Good News to those who are lost and dying. Once we have experienced His salvation, we will find ourselves telling everyone that we know Jesus personally. It's a special holy place to be, close to Jesus.

Don't let go of Him. Get to know Him. Talk to Him daily. Talk to Him about everything in your life.

—Audrey Rierson

Endurance

In selecting my Word, I fluctuated between choosing peace or endurance. Reflecting on my life today, I generally (although not always) have internal peace—like a cornerstone or anchor in my spirit and soul. But I need to work on endurance. When I give up—as so often I do, peace can evaporate like a sun-kissed morning mist temporarily from my soul...

My life patterns have been running away
when the heat gets turned up.
If I could not win, I stopped trying.
If there were a big fight with a loved one, I would take off.
The odd exception was my career where selfish ambition overrode
this tendency and kept me on the job!

At least, I am now cognizant of my weakness in these areas.
So "endurance," when I want to spiritually "leave town,"
is the word for me.

I wrote the above September 9, 2017, just a few weeks before the hardest trial of my life—when my beloved husband, Edward, was diagnosed with rare prostate cancer that had metastasized to his bones. I nursed him 24/7 for just less than four months when he passed into his Lord's arms. It seems the Lord knew beforehand precisely what word was suitable for me during these times!

That Thing (Plugged Up)

"On the last and greatest day of the festival,
Jesus stood and said in a loud voice,
"Let anyone who is thirsty come to me and drink.
Whoever believes in me, as Scripture has said, rivers
of living water will flow from within them."
John 7:37-38 (NIV)

Last week I was frustrated to find my sink backing up. After the water finally drained, a small residue of "dirt" remained in the sink. The plumber determined that the waste disposer was fine and that the blockage—**"that thing"**—was in an artery to the main water disposal pipe. I was so convinced that someone other than "Moi" must have been responsible for the problem by putting inappropriate waste down the disposal unit. My husband pointed out that I had been watering my fern in the sink daily and that dirt had overflowed when I did so. Oops, I was responsible for blocking my pipes!

In the same way on occasion, I might do the same thing with my spiritual pipes. **"That thing"** blocks the wonderful outpouring of living water—the Holy Spirit—flowing through me to others. And with it, some of the joy and peace that I generally experience flies out the window. And, who is responsible? It's not that other person who has offended me with **"that thing,"** or my husband who just said **"that thing again"** to irritate me, or that church person who has not done **"that thing"** to my liking? "Moi" again! If I have a "peeve," I am fretting over, and then I am blocking that wondrous flow of living water. I must endure, let it go, and stand complete in Christ.

What about you? Do you think you might plug up your spiritual outflows on occasion?

—Catherine Ricks Urbalejo

Enduring the Fiery Furnace

*"For the LORD your God is the one who goes with you to fight
for you against your enemies to give you victory."*
Deuteronomy 20:4 (NIV)

I was horrified. I shook with anger.
Tears of self-pity welled up in my eyes.
I wanted to scream out loud. Slam a door.
Throw a few things for good measure. I could not sleep!

Getting up out of bed, I marched angrily to the other bedroom. I did not wish to disturb my peacefully sleeping, and annoyingly oblivious husband with my tossing. There I was free to rant and rave in the fiery furnace of my mind. There was something that I did not like—that had offended me greatly. It rose in my mind to assume dark, gigantic, and grotesque proportions! I wanted to screech and shout, to rant and rave, to supposedly retake control of my life. I battled a long time in that fiery furnace wrestling with some dark unseen force. Back and forth, we went. Yes, I will voice my opinion and my anger. I will let it all hang out no matter the consequences! Why should I be treated this way! Never have I had such an epic struggle! But someone else was with me in that epic battle. Flashes, mere wisps of calm would penetrate the demon-possessed battlefield of my mind. Suddenly, with strength, I surely did not possess on my own, I made the correct moral choice. The sins that were trying to entangle me were cast off. Demons fled. Calm was then reestablished. I was convicted to return to the marriage bed and let the "horror" go.

Uncontrolled anger and the associated temptation to sin were overcome.
I had victoriously endured the fiery furnace!
Grace had surely had her way with me.
Peace readjusted herself in my soul.
I slept!

—Catherine Ricks Urbalejo

Patient Endurance

"Be joyful in hope, patient in affliction, faithful in prayer."
Romans 12:12 (NIV)

"Well, I said to myself I certainly blew that!"

I had just gotten entangled in the injustice and emotion of the moment and lost my temper with another soul regarding a neighborhood dispute. Angry, hurtful words erupted from my mouth in short staccato bursts.

The Spirit nudged me—I was convicted to shut my big loudmouth, albeit with heroic effort.

Now my anger redirected itself to the big insulted "Moi."

"What were you thinking?" I told myself crossly.

The Spirit, apparently not done with me yet, nudged again.

"What now?" I questioned, frustrated.

A thought trickled to the surface. *Was I still blowing it by being cross with myself?*

"Oops!" A major attitude change appeared to be in order.

Catherine, you have a choice, the idea whorled through my mind.

The inner voice was not letting up. It reminded me, that *choice is a fundamental gift of God to all mankind.*

Ah-ha went the rather slow grinding wheels of my mind; *I have the God-given ability to choose how I will respond to the offense. Will I choose patient endurance or rise like an agitated crow, feathers flying to wage a major war at the slightest insult?*

Wisdom speaks.

Choose patience. It will not be easy, but it is the right moral choice. I decide to select patience. *If I fail on occasion, I will pick myself up and continue the path set before me. I will endure patiently on the narrow way, strengthened by prayer and the joy of the blessed hope.*

—Catherine Ricks Urbalejo

Cloud of Witnesses

"Therefore, since we are surrounded by such a great cloud of witnesses,
let us throw off everything that hinders and the sin that so easily entangles.
And let us run with perseverance the race marked out for us."
Hebrews 12:1 (NIV)

One of my favorite poems by William Wordsworth contains the rhythmic prose:

"I wandered lonely as a cloud
That floats on high o'er vales and hills,
When all at once I saw a crowd,
A host, of golden daffodils;"

It reminds me of Hebrews 12:1—the reality that we are enveloped in a magnificent cloud, not of daffodils, but countless witnesses to Christ:

Prophets who foretold His coming as recorded in the Old Testament;
New Testament writers, who recorded His actual
birth, life, death, and resurrection;
Members of the body of Christ [believers], who by
their fruit testify to His spirit in them;
And, by God's glorious creation.
Do we hear and see this marvelous cloud? Or,
has familiarity blunted its impact?

Do I "wander lonely as a cloud" impervious to the presence of that magnificent cloud of witnesses, that surrounds me?

Or, am I of good cheer, my faith buoyed by the fact that our Lord has provided so strong a cloud of testimonies across generations?

With such evidence, surely, we are without excuse! Let us throw off our sins and turning our faces toward Jesus, persevere on the road He has set before us.

Having so endured to one day arrive gloriously at our promised eternal home!

—Catherine Ricks Urbalejo

Hold Firm

"Not that I have already obtained all this,
or have already arrived at my goal, but I press on to take
hold of that for which Christ Jesus took hold of me."
Philippians 3:12 (NIV)

A stranger saved my life.

I was sixteen and playing on a metal fence designed to prevent stupid people from falling into the raging sea far below. Stalwart embedded fence poles atop a 20-foot concrete seawall were built to keep the savage waves of the English Channel from eroding the shore. I slipped, managing to hang on to the lowest rail with my fingertips. Beneath me the water was sucked out rapidly in a dangerous undercurrent, making a roaring sound as it went. It was preparing to build into the next ferocious wave to hurl at the seawall battlements—this time with me in its sights. Me! I was to be smashed by its fury into a mangled pulp on the seawall.

Hanging onto the lower rail, I gazed with terror and pleading in my eyes at a young man above me—safely behind the fence. No words were spoken. He saw the horror on my face. He reached down. I grasped his hand. He raised me up. I was saved!

I don't think I even thanked him, this nameless stranger who saved my life. But I remember that event clearly, as if it were yesterday, though it's 55 years later. The trauma of my near-death experience is etched forever in my memory.

Many years later, another stranger saved my life. He put His hand out and reached down to me from heaven. I was dying in my sins, to be smashed by Satan unto death. This "stranger" offered the "free" gift of salvation—forgiveness of sins and eternal life. I reached up. With enduring love, He firmly took hold of my hand. This "stranger," Jesus Christ, is a stranger no more.

—Catherine Ricks Urbalejo

Row, Row, Your Boat

"But the one who looks into the perfect law, the law of liberty, and perseveres,
being no hearer who forgets but a doer who acts,
he will be blessed in his doing."
James 1:25 (ESV)

A new acquaintance was seated with me at my favorite eclectic coffee shop as I sipped my preferred and addictive green tea smoothie. No "en guarde" was experienced or difficulty in advancing the conversation—no stilted moments. Like friendly fencers, we pranced forward into lively dialogue, lunging and parrying gently with our easy volley of words. Time ticked by on greased wheels unheeded as if lubricated by the creamy satisfaction of my verdant-colored drink. Our lives spun by us. A kaleidoscope of memories burst forth then retreated as we shared with joy and sometimes tears, the stories of our many years—then a special moment!

I was chattering on with fervor about the need to be active, not passive in life—or as I put it—to row my boat. Passionately stating that if we are looking for a companion or soul mate, we cannot sit at home flopped in our chair like a wilted wallflower—prayerfully expecting God to dump one miraculously in our lap! We need to be proactive, get off our delicate rears out into the community, and **row our boats.**

To which my new friend nodded in agreement saying, "Yes indeed. There is a saying,

Pray, and row your boat."

Now, this was new to me—but, how it resonated deep in my spirit! Lyrical tones of "Michael, Row the Boat Ashore," echoed a tuneful melody in my brain. That brought back fond old memories of my father and myself attempting to sing this song together. As I ruminated on "pray and row your boat," it occurred to me how often I have rowed vigorously but left God out of the boat! Perhaps, that might explain metaphorically speaking, how when feverishly rowing my boat, I often capsize!

Pray and row your boat. Perhaps, you don't row your boat! Maybe, you do row your boat. But, do you pray and row your boat?

Through prayer— "May the God, who gives endurance…" (Romans 15:5 - NIV) guide you safely to shore.

—Catherine Ricks Urbalejo

The Key

"Jesus answered, 'I am the way and the truth and the life.'"
John 14:6 (NIV)

At times life can be a real pain—so hard to endure! I bow my head to pray. A vision comes to me:

In the palm of my sweaty left-hand rests what at first sight appears to be a smartphone. My swollen fingers with blood-red painted nails claw at this strange rectangular device. My hand tightens convulsively around it, then loosens as if unsure what to do with it. For this is no normal phone! Although the lower part is equipped with a standard screen, there the semblance of normality grinds to a halt. In the middle of the device is an enormous black keyhole and above it, covering one-third of the space, a window that seems to open out to nothing but blue skies. I am mystified. What can this mean?

I glance down at my right hand. To my surprise, I hold a giant red key between my trembling fingers. Perhaps, it will fit the lock, I muse. Suddenly, the lower screen erupts into a noisy and colorful profusion of current world events. Distracted from the key, I become ghoulishly immersed in this horror show—beheadings of Christians in the Middle East, an explosion in a gay bar in Florida, spewing body parts far and wide, a car mowing down innocents on a famous London bridge. This carnival of horrors continues. With a heroic effort of will, I push the button to "OFF, and the world recedes.

However, in the soothing silence, I become aware of a distant murmur. I strain my ears to hear it. The murmur becomes a persistent whisper. Now I can distinguish the elusive words.

"Jesus Christ is the Way, the Truth, and the Life."

The strange contraption seems to beckon me. I glance down at it, and the key begins to vibrate in my right hand as if calling my attention. A dawning realization—perhaps, this key may help solve this mystery. Slowly, the key becomes very heavy—I manage to insert it into the lock and turn it. I find myself transported to heavenly places—a gentle breeze caresses a rhapsody of purple and pink flowers shaking their heads in a merry dance. A gurgling stream flows through this lofty paradise. My soul sings. My spirit soars. I stroll toward eternity. Jesus is holding my hand. I come out of the vision with an abrupt start.

Clarification of this vision permeates my soul. Although we walk in this world often greatly saddened by its events and our circumstances, we have the key—Jesus Christ—to open the door to heaven and eternity. We must keep hold of that key—our eyes on Him. Let us not be distracted by the siren call of this world—for this world is temporary, and we look forward to our permanent home in heaven.

—Catherine Ricks Urbalejo

CHRIST IS THE KEY THAT GIVES STRENGTH TO ENDURE

Enduring Discipline

"It is for discipline that you have to endure. God is treating you as sons. For what son is there whom his father does not discipline?"
Hebrews 12:7 (ESV)

Being disciplined is not one of my favorite activities and probably not yours either.

Generally, God has disciplined me in subtle ways. Other times, He has taken a metaphorical baseball bat and knocked me over the head with it! Think about all the ways He might have disciplined you. Were you even aware of it or were you so busy, tied up in your life, that you missed God's gentle nudging? If you did notice, did you listen? Did you stop doing whatever it was, repent, and act to change your behavior?

In unpleasant circumstances or when experiencing undesirable emotions, I have learned (sometimes) to look at myself—to assess if God is trying to bring something to my attention. At times, I am just a blockhead!

Do I dislike someone because I am envious? The Holy Spirit will gently convict me of this sin. I should ask for forgiveness, change my attitude, look for positive traits in the person, and pray for them. Usually, I find the "dislike" fades into the past and no longer possesses such sharp elbows to jab me.

Have I charged into a situation on my "white horse of pride" to fix whatever is going on in my strength? Pride, as the old saying goes, usually goes before a great fall. Sure enough, God lets me tumble off my steed to "face plant" on the ground in front of my peers. The result—not only I but also others become aware of my puffery. That kind of discipline is tough—more like "baseball bat" correction! Better to pick myself up, dust myself off, apologize, and learn to be more humble, joyfully enduring the disciple of God as His child.

—Catherine Ricks Urbalejo

Angles and Tangles

"As iron sharpens iron, so one man sharpens another."
Proverbs 27:17 (NIV)

I was gazing at my view—islands in the sky—clusters of towering mountains springing from desert plains. Summits were reaching high into the purple haze of the atmosphere—their ink-like silhouette fingerprints for identification purposes. But if I look at them from different perspectives or angles, I am amazed at how they metamorphose into unrecognizable outlines. As an illustration, I am unable to distinguish my home range—the Whetstones in southern Arizona—if I observe them from a different perspective than my usual home-based view. If I were lost in a mountain range, it would be wise to ask someone knowledgeable of the area, which mountains they might be, and how I might get back on track.

The same is true from a spiritual point of view if I am lost in a particular situation. Perhaps, I need to look at the problem or circumstance from a different perspective. Reading the Bible may provide a solution, or perhaps the Holy Spirit has revealed a different "godly angle" to a fellow believer. I should be open to/or actively seek their counsel to resolve the tangle of a mess that I may have got myself into!

Sometimes, God may use me to offer wise words to another believer tangled up in their circumstances. God's Word teaches us that we are to sharpen one another. By providing a "different perspective" to a problem, we may help one another grow in God's will for our individual lives.

Sharing God-given words may be exactly what someone needs to hear while enduring the complexities of life.

—Catherine Ricks Urbalejo

Trust and Obey

"Lord Almighty, blessed is the one who trusts in you."
Psalm 84:12 (NIV)

When the world falls apart;
Please do not lose heart.
When you are sick and in pain;
Do not think it in vain;
For the Lord is beside you,
If you trust and obey.

*

When voices scream insults;
Life not going your way;
And fears overwhelm you;
Grasp tightly His hand;
And, walk in the light of His wonderful way,
Just trust and obey.

*

Fatigued beyond measure?
Read the Lord's treasure.
At the end of your rope?
Be refreshed by great hope.
For there is no other way,
Than to trust and obey.

—Catherine Ricks Urbalejo

Poisonous Fangs

"I say to God my Rock, "Why have you forgotten me?
Why must I go about mourning, oppressed by the enemy?"
Psalm 42:9 (NIV)

For twenty-five years, I suffered from depression, the antithesis of joy and peace. In my case, the consequence of self-imposed bad choices as the "Big I" marched through life and its pleasures, ignoring the guidance of childhood mentors to follow Christ. I usually put the needs of others after self—Christ was all but forgotten.

The bedrock of Christ's joy in my soul evaporated. The poisonous fangs of depression sunk deep into my soul. Sometimes it was even hard to move, to believe anything good about myself, even my brain seemed to stop functioning as if overwhelmed by a cloud of darkness. Satan laughed.

Have you experienced depression even if one wrought by the actions of others? Its fangs deplete your energy, numb your brain, and destroy your joy.

For an unbeliever or perhaps a backsliding Christian, a heroic effort must be made to throw this blood-sucking vampire off the back. Otherwise, it becomes nearly impossible to do so. If not, surely your spirit will sink into the blackest numbness of despair. A mental institution looms on the horizon. Suicide calls. For a believer, all things are possible with God. So, endure no matter where in the bottomless pit you may have sunk. Return to the Lord if you have backslidden. Make godly choices. Give your burdens to the Lord. Believe with all your heart that you, yes you, through Christ, have the strength to throw that depressive monster with its blood sapping fangs off your back. Endure, my friend, to see the glorious light at the end of this dark, oppressive tunnel appear!

—Catherine Ricks Urbalejo

Armageddon Within

"I know that nothing good lives in me, that is, in my sinful nature.
For I have the desire to do what is good, but I cannot carry it out. "
Romans 7:18 (NIV)

Awareness dawns slowly like the morning light at the birth of a new day.
Sin hides in the corridors of my body; its fleshly
tentacles at war with my rebirthed spirit.
Sometimes it retreats and hides; part of the submerged,
deadly iceberg of my unconscious
fleshly human nature.
Such is the constant state of the unbeliever;
blissfully ignorant or sometimes gleefully
tolerant of their inherent sinfulness.
Other times sin advances and I, with my new
nature, become conscious of the
gargantuan spiritual tug of war within. What a struggle ensues!
Sometimes with the grace of God, I overcome;
sometimes I perform a spiritual
"face plant."
What a miserable failure I can be!
My new nature desires to obey the moral law of
God but my sin nature, present since
my birth is at war with my new self.
But if I fall, I must pick myself up spiritually and continue the good fight.
I must finish the race as the apostle Paul commands.
God is gracious to forgive my failures if I have a repentant heart.
Satan and the world stand ready and able to egg
me on in pursuing these inwardly
birthed sinful pursuits.
But the Holy Spirit has convicted me of my sinful nature.
I know the enemy, and he is "me."
Knowing that sin skulks somewhere in my
putrid depths permits me to become
a watchman over my soul.
With God's strength, I will overcome this war within.

—Catherine Ricks Urbalejo

Ultimate Endurance – Our Role Model

"From noon until three in the afternoon darkness came over all the land.
About three in the afternoon Jesus cried out in a
loud voice, 'Eli, Eli, lema sabachthani?'
(which means 'My God, my God, why have you forsaken me?')"
Matthew 27:45-46 (NIV)

Two days before my husband died, ten months ago, the Lord brought into my life, my husband's eldest brother and nephew. As the old saying goes, *when one door shuts another door always opens.* His nephew lives near me. He and I are building a family relationship. God created us as an image of Himself. Just as He is a triune God (three persons in one) so we were built for connection and community. I pray that as each of us goes about their daily lives, we endure and build relationships that honor God

As we struggle, let us take hope in the ultimate endurance demonstrated by Jesus Christ. Taking on a physical body, He was obedient unto the cross where He willingly endured its agony and the fracture of his perfect relationship with His Father. The Bible tells us that God, Himself, turned away from the grotesque sin of the world that His Son bore on his body as the perfect sacrificial lamb for all time—once for all eternity. The enormity of how the Son suffered cannot be comprehended.

As believers, we have the assurance of a relationship with Christ and others, even when we suffer a loss. And, we have the blessed hope that death is not the end.

—Catherine Ricks Urbalejo

Words in Due Season

Let **Peace** blossom as the internal fruit of our souls,
Expect God to work good in all our circumstances,
Be **relentless** in godly pursuits; keep your word,
Do not faint at the challenges of life, set godly boundaries
and be **overwhelmed** by the spirit of God,
Take joy that you have **found** the Lord your God,
Encourage all those who God puts in your way
with a friendly word or act of kindness,
Be **quiet** and listen for that still small voice,
Let your spirit take flight with the beautiful **music** of God's creation,
Seek wisdom and **understanding** for these are better than gold and silver,
Watch to see what He will do; be alert—the watchman of your soul,
Have a **heart** for the Lord and others. Love them with all your heart,
Let **faith** grow stronger day by day—belief in Him,
Let Christ be your **source**, your rock, the lamp of your salvation,
And, in all these let us **endure** to finish the race set before us.

—Catherine Ricks Urbalejo

Women of Grace Writers

Juanita Adamson is retired from Federal service. She has been in children's ministry for over 20 years, teaching Sunday School, Little "Kidz" church, and Missionettes. She has written and directed several dramas, including her church's yearly Christmas presentation of "Walk Thru Bethlehem." She volunteers as a Court Appointed Special Advocate (CASA), at the Life Care Center, and the Salvation Army. She enjoys crafts, writing and directing dramas, music, reading, and outdoor adventures.

Sonya Andres is married to the love of her life, Scott Andres. They both praise God for leading them to the Mountain View Assembly of God Church. God has prepared Sonya for the Women of Grace writing ministry by previous roles as Women's Director, teaching Women's Bible Studies, and retiring from 28 years of Information Technology. By the Grace of God, she has become an Author, which still gives her Holy Bumps!

Phyllis Andrews retired in 1995 from a very successful career with the Federal Government in Washington, DC, after 30 years of service and before moving to Arizona. She has been privileged to serve the Church for many years through various music and teaching ministries. Her passions include her family and her service as coordinator for the care center ministry and the Women of Grace Writers. She has also participated with her husband in his work as a pastor and teacher and jail and prison ministries.

Paula J. Domianus praises God for her loving husband Ralph of forty years. They are active members of First Christian Church in Sierra Vista, where she is currently the administrative assistant. Her passion is Missions and Outreach Ministries. She loves spending time in her prayer garden, with family, friends, and their dog, Shelby. Paula adores writing and is a published poet.

Karen Furukawa considers it a privilege to have traveled and lived all over the United States and overseas with her husband, a military officer (retired.)She homeschooled her two sons, worked in Office Administration, taught Sunday school, VBS, and Women's Bible Study. She loves writing as an outlet and to point people to The Living God.

Carmen Mosher has been in pastoral ministry with her husband Allan for over 35 years. They currently are serving in Silver Springs, NV. She is a mother of two and grandmother of seven. She loves all things "wordy:" Reading, writing, teaching and speaking, and prays that in all her wordy endeavors, God is glorified!

Audrey Rierson has lived in Arizona for twenty-nine years. Audrey started writing after the death of her husband in 2006. She stays busy with crafts and personalized greeting cards. Many special friends join her at Bible studies, writing groups, and community functions. Her daughter Lynn and grandson Cody keep her busy in her spare time and give her lots of material to write about.

Catherine Ricks Urbalejo was born in England and came to the United States in 1970. She attended Michigan State University obtaining a Ph.D. in Nutritional Biochemistry followed by a 30-year career in the Agricultural Sector developing new products for livestock. Her hobbies are writing, horseback riding, camping in an RV, and downhill skiing. She is a Colson Fellow graduate since May 2019 and is an active member of her local church. She is widowed with one son and three wonderful grandchildren.

Millie Wasden grew up in Sherman Oakes, California. Following a challenging childhood marred by severe dyslexia, attention deficit disorder, and parental loss, Millie was able to graduate from high school and became a dental assistant. In 1966 she married Sterling Wasden, and God blessed them with two beautiful children. Sterling's mother brought Millie to the Lord in 1964— the fulfillment of a childhood desire. She now resides in Sierra Vista has been a Princess House Lifestyle Consultant for 20 years.

Contributing Authors

Cynthia Harris Beckwith is an Arizona transplant from South Carolina, by way of the US Army. She is the 2nd eldest of six siblings. Cynthia's father is a retired minister. She has two children—a daughter, Bambi Rose, in South Carolina, and a son, Matthew, who lives in Sierra Vista. She has six grandchildren. She has been the store manager of the local Dollar Tree for the past eight years. Cynthia enjoys reading and writing short stories and poetry. She also enjoys relaxing with her husband Jimmy and their dog, Jake.

Olivia Brant is a word lover who enjoys her secretarial job but would prefer to be reading! Olivia's words can be found monthly on the _Mountain View_ blog at _www.mvaog.com_ or occasionally on her blog, _LivGrace_ at _www.livgracefull. blogspot.com._ Her writings are also included in _The Women of Grace Writers_ first book, _Reflections: Our View from the Mountain._

Terry Hunt Crowley was raised on an isolated ranch in northern Arizona. She grew up loving animals and the outdoors. She married a cowboy and lived on several ranches where she gave her heart to Jesus. Terry and her husband, Dan, raised five children and now work their cattle in northern Arizona. Terry is also an accomplished photographer of Arizona scenery.

Reverend Rebecca Fiedler has worked in the church in capacities which include Sermons, Prayer Team Leader, Adult Sunday School, Choir Director, and Soloist. Her education includes Master of Music, BA in Bible, BA in Church Music, Berean's Ministerial Studies Level One Certificate, and Indiana Christian University's One Year Certificate.

Diane Johnson is retired from Sierra Vista Unified School District and is the current owner of the lady's fashion boutique, Style 161. She grew up in Southern California and became a born-again Christian at the age of 21. Feeling called to some form of ministry, Diane attended California Baptist University for two years. As a wife of a Marine, she traveled to North Carolina. While there, she served as a youth director in the local Baptist church. She moved to AZ almost 30 years ago and has taught numerous Bible studies and have been involved in various women's ministries.

Pat Olson lives in Sierra Vista, Arizona with her husband Dave and her sweet rescue pup Scruffy. They have three grown children and eight grandchildren, whom she adores. They are a retired military family, enjoy traveling, running a business, and enjoy fellowship with believers across the miles.

Rosemary Raptis grew up in Charlton, MA; she now lives in Worcester, MA. She lived in Arizona for four years and taught Children's Ministry, Missionettes, and intercessory prayer. Rosemary has three children; her oldest daughter died at 37. She has also lost two husbands. She has three grandchildren. Painting is her hobby.

Alan Reed is the oldest son of one of the *Women of Grace Writers,* Phyllis Andrews. Alan is an Associate Minister at his local church in Upper Marlboro, MD, where he serves as a certified Life Coach, Praise & Worship Leader, Drama Ministry, and as a Bible Institute teacher/facilitator. He has also worked as a Music Educator for the past 26 years in Maryland, Washington, D.C., and Virginia.

Kristine Richardson is the daughter of Women of Grace Writer Millie Wasden. She received an AA degree before transferring to Cal Poly San Luis Obispo, CA, where she studied Ornamental Horticulture, which led to her becoming a floral designer. In 2009 she started her business designing jewelry and accessories. Her work is at KristinesKreations.com and DivaKreations.etsy. com. After living in CA her whole life, God moved Kristine and her husband to GA in 2015 where they have recently been blessed to purchase a new home.

Sharon Rustia received Jesus as Savior at age 13. She got serious about the Lord after the birth of her two daughters, whom she wanted to raise according to God's ways. Sharon homeschooled her girls for years until they entered public high school. Sharon has also served in Primary Church and Women's Ministries.

David Sherman is a pastor who sees God in every living thing and sometimes things that are not alive. Discovering God and sharing His love with others through his writing are his passion. David lives in the White Mountains of Arizona with his wife, Tina, and Jenny, his dog. He has published two books, "Learning to Agalliao" (Publisher-Westbow Press) and "What My Dog Taught Me About Jesus (Publisher-Xlibris)."

**Wannetta Wagner** has a passion for bringing belief, hope, and inspiration to others, and facilitate freedom and transformation from the lies that hold people in bondage. Her heart's desire is to love others back to life with the unconditional love of Jesus Christ. She currently serves as an International Master Coach for Global Entrepreneur's Institute that facilitates Kingdom Principles and Values based on the book of Proverbs to students internationally.

End Notes

1 **The Absence of Peace** [page 3] - https://www.imdb.com/title/tt62179581

2 **Impossible to Keep Quiet** [page 67] - https://en.m.wikipedia.org/wiki/ I%27II_ Fly _Away

3 **The B-I-B-L-E** [page 78] - www.kididdles.com/lyrics/b120.html

4 **The B-I-B-L-E** [page78] - The Gideons International New Testament with Psalms and Proverbs. Copyright 1985,1983 by Thomas Nelsen, Inc.

5 **A Father's Love** [page 83] - wikipedia.org/wiki/Billy_Boy

6 **Heavenly Mission** [page 86] - https://en.wikipedia.org/wiki/Amazing Grace

7 **Heavenly Mission** [page 86] - www.brainyquote.com/authors/martin luther

8 **Sing Praises to His Greatness** [page 87] - wikipedia.org/How Great thou Art

9 **A Matter Of Minutes** [page 88] - CHASING THE WIND - The National Library of Poetry ISBN 1-57553-574-2 pg. 212

10 **A Matter Of Minutes** [page 88] - wikipedia.org/wiki/Category: Stuart_Hamblen_songs

11 **A Matter Of Minutes** [page 88] - Sun Writers of Southern Arizona-WORDS-Pondering Moments Volume 1 Issue 4 Date November 1998

12 **Quest** [page 89] - Sun Writers of Southern Arizona-WORDS-Pondering Moments Volume1 Issue 2 Date September 1998

13 **Quest** [page 90] - lyrics.fandom.com/wiki/Chris_Tomlin: Forever

14 **Follow Me** [page 93] - Wikipedia.org/Ira Stanphill

15 **Watch The** Pot [page 99] – TAKE THE LID OFF by Smokie Norful, Thomas Nelson, 2017, ISBN 0718078734

16 **For Heaven's Sake** [page 105] - https://www.umcdiscipleship.org/resources/ history-of-hymns-his-eye-is-on-the-sparrow

17 **To The Very End** [page 120] - Author: Anne Graham Lotz, My Heart's Cry, pg. 148

18 **A Soft Power** [page 121] - Author: Oswald Chambers, My Utmost for His Highest, from the Devotional for August 21 (no page numbers)

19 **A Soft Power** [page 121] - Author: Charles R. Swindoll, Growing Strong in the Seasons of Life, pg. 316

20 **In Good Standing** [page 126] - www.annegrahamlotz.org

21 **Our Enemy** [page 131] - Author: John Eldredge, Wild at Heart, (page number unknown)

"Let the words of my mouth and the meditation of my heart
Be acceptable in Your sight, O LORD, my strength and my Redeemer."
Psalm 19:14 (NKJV)

To purchase Hardback/Paperback or E-Book copies, please contact:
Westbow Press
A Division of Thomas Nelson & Zondervan
www.Bookstore.westbowpress.com Phone: 866-928-1240
and through
Women of Grace Writers Facebook Page
https://www.facebook.com/wogwriters

~ ~ ~ ~ ~

For information on the Women of Grace Writers, please contact:
Mountain View Assembly of God
Attn. Sonya Andres
102 N. Colombo Ave., Sierra Vista, AZ 85635
Phone: 520-458-0487
mtviewaog@mvaog.com or womenofgracewriters@gmail.com

Printed in the United States
By Bookmasters